WF-BUF-5TQ

Is There Bacon in Heaven?

A MEMOIR

ALI HASSAN

Published by Simon & Schuster

New York   London   Toronto   Sydney   New Delhi

SIMON &
SCHUSTER
CANADA

Simon & Schuster Canada
A Division of Simon & Schuster, Inc.
166 King Street East, Suite 300
Toronto, Ontario M5A 1J3

This Simon & Schuster Canada edition September 2022

SIMON & SCHUSTER CANADA and colophon are trademarks of Simon & Schuster, Inc.

For information about special discounts for bulk purchases, please contact Simon & Schuster Special Sales at 1-800-268-3216 or CustomerService@simonandschuster.ca.

Manufactured in the United States of America

10 9 8 7 6 5 4 3 2 1

Library and Archives Canada Cataloguing in Publication
Title: Is there bacon in heaven? : a memoir / Ali Hassan.
Names: Hassan, Ali (Actor), author.
Description: Simon & Schuster Canada edition.
Identifiers: Canadiana (print) 20210181516 | Canadiana (ebook) 20210181583 | ISBN 9781982149178 (softcover) | ISBN 9781982149185 (ebook)
Subjects: LCSH: Hassan, Ali (Actor) | LCSH: Comedians—Canada—Biography. | LCSH: Actors—Canada—Biography. | LCSH: Muslims—Canada—Biography. | CSH: Pakistani Canadians—Biography. | LCGFT: Autobiographies.
Classification: LCC PN2308.H38 A3 2022 | DDC 792.7/6028092—dc23

ISBN 978-1-9821-4917-8
ISBN 978-1-9821-4918-5 (ebook)

For my mom—You were an angel.

For my dad—I tried not to end any of my sentences with a preposition.

Contents

CONTENTS

Is There Bacon in Heaven?

INTRODUCTION

THERE ARE A FEW TIMES in my life when I've felt truly cornered.

Once, when I was in high school, an older boy named Nils saw the Moosehead Beer baseball hat I was wearing and said to me, "Moosehead? More like moose *piss*." Now, the smart move would have been to nod and say, "Thank you for your input, sir," because when I say Nils was an older boy, I actually mean that he was a younger man. He had the build of a fully formed twenty-eight-year-old pugilist and the vibes of a kid who had never been hugged by his father. He was also apparently a teen who was doing beer tastings in his spare time.

I, however, wasn't notorious for making smart moves. In my defence, my hat represented a brewery from my birth province, New Brunswick, and I had spent my *own money* (huge deal) on it just days earlier. I was walking into school with new "duds" on, and this guy was already disrespecting them before first recess. And so, without thinking, I quickly retorted, "That's pretty weird that you know what moose piss tastes like, Nils." I don't know if it was the response itself or the fact that some younger kid thought he could call him by his first name, but the more important point is that Nils had his hand around my neck, and my feet raised off the ground by about half a foot, within seconds. Nils really wasn't seeing this as the Canadian Heritage Moment it could have been. His buddy—also a Brown guy (et tu, Darius?)—was standing right beside Nils, smirking and revelling in the moment. I was certain my near future belonged in the nurse's office or a hospital, until two angelic female friends of

Nils started saying, "Nils, come on, put him down" and "Don't be mean." He looked at the girls, he looked at me, and as quickly as it had all begun, I was deemed to not be worth his time and dropped back to the ground.

Another time, in my twenties, my friends and I left a nightclub at 3 a.m. in Montreal, only to find out that there was some kind of police operation happening outside and blocking traffic on the street. This meant that my friend's car, parked right outside the club—a spot I had referred to as "preordained" when he reversed into it four hours prior—was now in the worst place possible. It was also then that I realized how badly I needed to pee. I circled ten feet back to the club I had just left and asked the bouncer if I could quickly use the bathroom. "No." But man, I was just in here—look at the stamp that is almost still visible on my wrist. "No." Buddy, I spent many dollars here tonight and now the liquid your establishment provided me with wants out—wouldn't it be the decent thing for you to let a grown man back inside for one minute so that he doesn't have to publicly wet his pants? "No one gets back inside." With my negotiating powers having met their match, I started contemplating my options. That is to say, I looked at the corner of a parking lot and walked toward it. In retrospect, I really underestimated the capacity of the Montreal police to multitask that night. While they were knee-deep in "Operation Close the Street," a pair of officers were also able to drive up behind me and shine their bright police light on my back as I stood, cornered, peeing in a literal corner. While this incident did not end in any pants-wetting, it did end with me being handed a $120 ticket for *Urination Publique*.

And, more recently, as a father, I felt that same cornered feeling when my oldest son, at age four, approached me as I sat at the kitchen table quietly minding my own business.

Him: Papa.

Me: Yes.

Him: Are you Muslim?

Me: What the— Of course I'm Muslim, kiddo! You know *that*! I'm just like all of you. We're all Muslim.

Him: Do we go to the mosque?

Me: Errr . . . Well, no. You would have noticed if we were going to the mosque.

Him: How come we don't go to the mosque?

Me: Okay, do you want to go to the mosque? I can ask your grandmother to take you—

Him: How come *you* don't go to the mosque?

Me: Look, it's complicated. I'm not a practising Muslim. I'm more like a freelancer, you know? They call and say, "We need you at the mosque," and I say, "I was kind of hoping to work from home today." You know what I mean?

Him: Do you drink *beard*?

Had this taken place in a courtroom, at this point is where a lawyer might have called me a "hostile witness." I started to panic and called for my wife immediately. It's not that I had anything against my son's very normal, reasonable questions. I didn't even have anything against his mispronunciation of "beer." What was stressing me out was that he sounded like an adult, and I sounded like the same confused kid I was for most of my life—unsure of my connection to Islam.

The fact is, for a lot of my youth, I thought of myself as a white guy. I knew ten Blue Rodeo songs by heart, I played ice hockey, I used a Crock-Pot. Y'know, a white guy! I was the sum of my experiences, and for long stretches of time those experiences were stereotypically "white." A day of skiing followed by some "Irish coffee" by the fireplace, anyone? Don't mind if I do! There were times, early in my life, at least, that I felt so unaware of my own skin colour that if someone had yelled, "Paki!" I might have even looked around and said, "Really? Where?"

Strangely, at various times in my life I was also an honorary Trinidadian, Goan, Parsi, and Sikh. I can still hear my mother yelling, "You're an honorary everything, except a Muslim Pakistani!" I know, Mom—things get complicated when you're desperate to belong.

Much like my spiritual life, my work life also would have been best summed up as a series of bad choices eventually leading to a series of pretty good situations. The culmination of bad professional choices came in the late nineties when I decided to make the ultimately unwise choice of becoming an IT consultant. "Becoming" feels like much too strong a word here. Even "consultant" is misleading. I mean, it was certainly my title. It was right there on my business card. But anyone who worked with me would tell you it was a title *in name only*. And I'm not the victim of some scheme here. No one put a gun to my head and demanded that I spend $22,000 on a degree that would give me the credentials to work in the IT field. This was a CHOICE. I had been kicked out of an MBA program and had no idea what to do with my life; I looked at my groups of close friends and thought, *Who among ye is dumb, and yet successful? Oh, there's a few of them. And they're all in IT! I should get into IT!* A worse rationale for a career path has yet to be devised. It ended in failure, as it should have. Although, it did give me the opportunity to live and play (and *eat*—so much eating) in Chicago for a year and a half. Then 9/11 precipitated my move back to my parents' home in Montreal, posthaste, and I finally found myself looking for work in the food world: truly, the only world I ever cared about. Yes, that's something I should have thought about before applying for that loan. I became an in-his-parents'-basement-dwelling self-trained chef, a caterer, and a cooking instructor (mostly in grocery stores). And despite all these jobs, I still managed to live well below the poverty line for many years. Not knowing a damned thing about how to run a business helped. But I had never been happier. "Do what you love," *is it?*

Whereas religion continued to be a source of great confusion, work became clearer over the years. I added stand-up comedy, another passion, to my list of careers. TWO passions—imagine the nerve of this guy? Eventually, I was a chef, a stand-up comedian, *and* a radio broadcaster.

A few years ago, my religion, my chef background, my stand-up comedy chops, and my notoriety from broadcasting all collided. More accurately, I experienced one of the most un-Islamic things I could have ever imagined. I got an email from Toronto Ribfest asking if I would consider being one of their celebrity judges. Just to be clear: the largest, most pork-friendly event in all of Canada asked a guy named Ali Hassan if he would judge some of the aforementioned pork at said event. Further clarification: eating pork is regarded as one of the greatest sins for Muslims. So, Ribfest clearly did no research on Ali Hassan, or on Islam, or on religion in general.

Long story short, I accepted their invitation.

To paraphrase the Dos Equis Most Interesting Man in the World: *I don't eat ribs often, but when I do, it's at Ribfest.* My first Ribfest was on a glorious day, too. The sun was a-shinin'. The ribs were a-grillin'. I was clearly excited. So excited, in fact, that the organizer of the festival felt compelled to come over and say, "Ali, this is your first time here, so I just want to warn you that there will be sixteen competitors this year. In other words, there will be a lot of ribs coming to you in a short period of time. *We recommend* that you just take a small piece, taste it, mark your score, and quickly move on." I've never been a fan of authority, and this woman had just given the wrong suggestion to the wrong man. *This is the greatest day of my life, lady! I'll show you!* And, in a sense, I did. I ate every morsel of every rib that came my way. But I was also reminded that maybe I should be more open to suggestions. By the eleventh pair of ribs, as I was starting to crumple in great discomfort, I thought to myself, *THIS is why these are banned in my religion!*

Now, I don't really mind having the rep of a Muslim Ribfest judge. I came to terms many years ago with the fact that I am a cultural Muslim. The problem now is that I have kids. Wait, that doesn't sound right. I have four wonderful kids! I was a single, unmarried idiot, and I went from zero kids to four kids in four years. Not a journey I would necessarily recommend to anyone else, mind you. I met my daughters over a decade ago—they came into my life as part of a beautiful package with my wife. And then we had two boys. And then I got a vasectomy. But I digress.

It's a lot of kids and a lot of questions. And a lot of confusion. Most of which is my own. How can a guy who judged at a Ribfest (three years in a row, by the way) credibly talk to his kids about being a Muslim, never even mind a "good" Muslim! Furthermore, my own knowledge is pretty rusty. I am woefully unprepared to answer a lot of what they ask.

My girls never really asked me questions about Islam. I don't believe it has anything to do with their lack of inquisitiveness. I think they were just astute enough to take one look at me and realize, *This guy doesn't have any of the answers*. My boys lack this astuteness and test my knowledge regularly.

Granted, it must be confusing for the kids to watch Papa in action. Maybe I look inconsistent at best, hypocritical at worst. But truthfully, I've never been more comfortable with who I am. But it took *years*. Years of self-discovery, self-doubt, judgement, embarrassment, and even experiences with discrimination and racism for me to become the "Cultural Muslim" that I am.

You can't choose where and to whom you're born. You can't choose how those people raise you. And you don't choose who you meet along the way—the unlikely influences that will help shape and steer you. But eventually, with some planning and dumb luck, you find your way. And if you're really lucky, you fall in love with the path that you've carved for yourself.

The challenge is, you can't just hand over *all that* to a kid. And so, I share my story. I hope it helps.

Part 1

HUMBLE BEGINNINGS

Chapter 1

IT'S NOT FAIR

I'VE HAD PEOPLE TELL ME throughout my life, periodically, that I'm not a good Muslim. It's always nice when people take time out of their day to give you unsolicited feedback. And sure, you *could* argue that I'm not a "good Muslim," I suppose. But truthfully, you're not even picking up on half of what I'm putting down. I'm not even a good *Brown guy*. Not because I don't want to be. This isn't an act of defiance. I just have a variety of what you might call "congenital limitations."

A number of years ago, we went to Jamaica with a few friends and their kids. As my son Maaz was walking around the pool playing nervously with his hands, he caught the eye of my friend Pulak, who is a physiotherapist. He pulled my son over, made him do a variety of stretches, and concluded that the boy likely has "generalized joint hypermobility." Immediately my wife and I were like, "Is that bad? 'Cause it sounds bad." While there are some real concerns attached to this condition, in short, he's too flexible. So, he'll be the guy at parties who pulls his thumb back so far that his thumbnail touches his wrist, and creepy stuff like that. Allegedly, it's a "hereditary" condition? No. Nothing could be further from the truth.

I have never been flexible. A great source of shame for me is that I can't sit cross-legged. Many people struggle to believe that because (a) it's something that kindergarten students do, and (b) in South Asian culture, that's how we sit *all the time*. Indian or Pakistani families will have twelve chairs in their home, and they'll invite thirty-five people over. Guests will happily find an open space

9

on the ground and bend themselves into a neat pretzel. I cannot do this. The most I can do is sit on my butt, grab my knees toward my chest, grimace, and rock back and forth—basically, the pose you see in movies after someone has been bullied and beat up in an alley.

For the past two decades, my primary New Year's resolution has been "to become flexible." It used to involve me starting my day by doing some horrendously unflattering stretches in my underwear for twenty minutes. If you were to look through my window in the morning, first you'd feel ill, and then you'd wonder, "Is this guy training to be a hockey goalie?" My stretching regime involved pretty much every position a goalie might use to make a save. I'd start with the "splits"—getting my pelvis down as low as almost three feet from the ground—and then move into all kinds of wild twists and turns, ending with lying on my back and stretching my legs out "spread eagle" style. I can hear you saying, "Please, Ali, tell us more and spare no detail," but I think I'll move on before the book requires an EXPLICIT CONTENT stamp on its cover.

Whatever my exact stretching routine might have been, the more important point is that every year, by late January, I quit the whole thing, discouraged by the pain and disconcerted by what sounded like old stairs creaking and coming loose in my knees and hips. In recent years, I've solicited my children's help, asking them to stand on one knee each as I try to sit cross-legged. Only in this way can I approximate the feeling of being a normal Brown guy for a few minutes.

At one point in my life, when I was exploring the musical side of my cultural roots, I took tabla lessons. The tabla, if you're not familiar, is a pair of percussion instruments that sit on the ground and are played with the hands. One drum is slightly larger—it's the bass drum that you play using your fingers and the heel of your palm. The smaller drum is used for treble and tonal sounds and played with the fingers of your other hand. And tabla drums are heavy. I mention that because my cousin Zaki brought them in his suitcase for me from Pakistan—his back ached for a month. And when I used to lug them the twenty blocks to my lessons, my bag would leave red strap marks across my clavicle for hours. But it was worth it, because I loved everything about that instrument. Its sound is unlike any other percussion instrument I've ever heard.

One way to play tabla is to sit cross-legged with the drums in front of you. Actually, I was quickly informed that this is the *only* way to play them. Apparently, my seated flying-V style was too unorthodox for my teacher. And my wrapping-my-legs-around-the-tabla technique didn't do much for him, either. I remember in our third or fourth lesson, he was on his tabla teaching our group of five students some notes to play. I was keenly sitting right in front of him and mimicked the same movement with my hands, playing the notes back to him. I asked, "What do you think?" But he wasn't looking at my hands or listening to the notes I had just played (perfectly, by the way). He was staring at my wide-open legs, in complete disgust. I'll never forget his words: "I can't. I just can't." Sigh. I'm pretty sure that was my last tabla lesson. Or rather, my musical exploration was put on hiatus, until I learned to sit cross-legged. The hiatus, twenty years later, continues. If you're reading this, Ritesh—I'm sorry, man. Were it not for the inflexibility, I really think I coulda been a contender.

I have resorted out of desperation to taking the occasional yoga class to make my body as springy and pliant as it should be by nature. A few years ago, I was taking a class with a woman named Michelle from Thunder Bay, Ontario. I used to spend most of the class imagining what her perspective of me must have been. She leaves her small town, gets immersed in Indian culture, picks up some of the language, gets an appreciation for some of the customs, learns the Ayurvedic traditions, trains for years to become a yoga instructor—only to one day meet a Brown man in her class who can't cross his legs. Every class she'd tell me, "Stretch . . . Breathe . . . Oh, you're sweating *a lot*, Ali—are you okay? Good . . . Now let's start our *Surya Namaskar*."

All I could do every class to feel any better about myself was mutter under my breath, "That's not how that's pronounced." I'm not sure I really knew how it was pronounced, but her way didn't sound right. "And now, let's begin the *Surya Namaskar* . . ." No, *you* begin the *"Surya Namaskar"* and *I* am going to pray that I haven't torn anything important!

One year, I took a family yoga class with my wife and daughters. The girls were under ten—still at the age when they think their parents might be kind of cool. That all went out the window, thanks to the class. I was sweating and groaning so much that my own family kept shifting their mats away from me. By the third class, the three of them were in different corners of the studio, each pretending not to know who I was. That was my last time in a yoga studio.

I remember as a young man being at Indian and Pakistani house parties and seeing my father beside me, cross-legged and leaning forward to eat food from a plate that was a foot in front of him. *A foot in front of him!* Why was it that Faruq Hassan could sit cross-legged and effortlessly lean forty-five degrees forward, while his progeny was doing everything in his power not to naturally tip backward? I would try to copy my father's moves, struggling to reach one hand way in front of me to get to my plate. I could just barely do it, but my hands were so shaky—my entire body was trying not to come apart—and my face was so far back that inevitably a curry of some kind would spill on the carpet, on my socks, or on my pants before the fork reached my mouth. My dad would just look at me, shake his head, and laugh. *Dude—why is this happening? I come from you! And you come from where yoga was invented. Shouldn't there be some residual benefit to that? Did you adopt me from a white couple? I WANT ANSWERS!*

I wish my non-flexibility was my only issue. Even worse is the fact that I sunburn. Here's the thing: I am Pakistani. Once upon a time, Pakistan was part of India. In fact, we have a date: It was *all the time* before August 14, 1947. South Asians call this time pre-partition—there was no Pakistan, just India. The good old days, right? I'm kidding! (Am I kidding? Who knows? I'll leave that one out there.) My dad was born in India, in a city that later became part of Pakistan. My mom was also born in India, in Delhi. And yet, despite having parents who come from the Indian subcontinent, I sunburn. Where's the justice?! There are certain advantages to being a Pakistani, and not burning up in the sun should absolutely be one of them. I have freckles on my face! On WebMD, freckles are described as "something that people with fair skin or red hair are most likely to have." How is it that I quite literally have more in common with a redheaded Irish lass than I do with my own people? To this day, thoughtful birthday gifts for me include cheese, money, and tubes of sunscreen that are SPF 65 or higher.

Crueller still is that my arms get very dark in the summer, but only my arms. It's a nice sight if I'm ever poolside: a slightly bronzed head ending abruptly at the neck, nearly black hands and arms, and then a body exhibiting various shades of pale, pasty, and red. A classic "farmer's tan," if you will. And by the way, there's *no* farming going on in my family. Not now, and not in my ancestry, either. Sometimes in summer, on the rare occasion when I'm wearing short shorts, I will rest my black hands on my white thighs and my wife will say it looks like I'm in a biracial relationship with myself.

I suppose the silver lining is that by the middle of winter I am finally a uniform, head to toe, deep shade of grey. One February, someone asked me if I was Polish, just to give you an idea of the situation. And *they* were Polish.

If you're wondering if my inflexibility and skin issues are genetic—no, both my parents bent appropriately in all the right places. Dad had a greyish-brown thing going on and my mother looked every bit like you might imagine a "Yasmin Hassan" would—a nice uniform brown.

From a genetic perspective, observing my dad was actually an exercise in self-loathing, and not just because he could sit comfortably in any position. My father had the strongest teeth I'd ever seen—perfectly straight, and he could rip the skin off stalks of sugarcane. Have you ever seen sugarcane? This is a crop that helps boost the annual sales of machetes. I never saw this, but I'm convinced that he was one of those people who could crack open a beer bottle with his teeth. *My* teeth, you may ask? A bloody mess (especially after I floss). My bottom teeth look like a blind drunkard erected a fence along the gums, and I've had three crowns put in before the age of forty-five. The last time I cracked a tooth, it was from some "very chewy bread." I am losing the survival of the fittest on a daily basis.

My dad had long hair, and pretty much all of it, well into his sixties. I started to bald at twenty-one. When I started losing my hair—or at least became aware of my hair loss—is when I truly realized, *Okay, we can't let up on this personality thing, buddy. One will need to overcompensate for one's shortcomings.*

When you bald early, it's not just the hair loss that hurts; you also come to realize that most of your friends are horrible people. I suspected myself of having thinning hair on the back of my head, and every time I asked my friends if I was losing my hair, they would say, "No, no, it looks fine!" Who is that helping? Eventually I *will* get hold of a second mirror! One of my friends actually said, "Don't worry, you're tall enough that no one will notice." WHAT THE. You know that I sit down from time to time, right?

"Hey, Ali, can you pick up that book I just dropped?"
"Oh, no can do. I'm off bending over forever."
"It's literally just between your feet."
"Nope, can't let my dirty balding secret out. Tell you what, I'll
    just kick it to you and hope it gets some air."

And when I finally did get a look at my scalp, it was like a blueberry pancake back there! The pancake batter being my white scalp and the blueberries the little patches of hair stubbornly holding on for dear life. It even looked like there was maple syrup glistening on the back of my head, but that was just sweat because of how nervous I was to be balding.

Also, my dad had no body hair. I'm gonna say he had a total of ten hairs in a tiny patch on his chest. Meanwhile, I resemble a furry stuffed animal— everywhere *except* for my head.

And my father would *never* sweat! He would be in the garden in our backyard, complaining about how "bloody hot" it was but not sweating a drop. We all knew that if he was sweating, it was time to call for help because he was probably having a cardiac episode. Meanwhile, I sweat profusely from sniffing a spicy bowl of soup, taking a brisk walk in September, or having a tense conversation. My father was also a voracious reader, plowing through two books a week, on top of all the other work he did. My eyes would start to ache after reading an *Archie's Double Digest*.

With respect to hair, teeth, and eyes, I got all the genes from my mom's side. Her bald father and brother paved a path for me to start balding early in life, I just cracked my third adult tooth, and I've been wearing glasses since my teens. The unfairness is almost too painful to talk about.

On the other side of things, my mother was a model of moderation. She never drank alcohol—and as my Trinidadian buddy Dave would say, "She doesn't drink? So she have a REALLLL drinkin' problem!" She set out time to exercise a little bit almost every day, never overate, and never even drove fast. Do you think I got *any* of that? I thought I was auditioning for *The Fast and the Furious* every time I got in a car, I have been overweight since my teens, and I can't remember a meal where I didn't get up and say, "Ooh, shouldn't have had that second plate." (Fine, third plate.)

My mother never got the diabetes and heart disease that my father did, so sometimes I think that maybe, just maybe, those genes will come my way. But then I remember the way I've eaten and drunk for the last thirty years, and I try to think about something else.

I guess none of us can control what we get from our parents, and it was always pretty clear that I got the wrong stuff from the wrong one. But where nature failed, nurture was there to pick up some of the pieces.

My parents met in Pakistan and then came together from Pakistan to Leeds, UK, and from Leeds to New Brunswick, Canada. You know, *that* old cliché. My dad was a fan of reading from a young age, and his plan—once it was fully clear that he had no aptitude for the sciences—was to get a master's degree in literature and then somehow work in that field. There were no vision boards at the time, so I think this is as far as the original plan went. The story goes that there was one short detour: he decided to join his friend Saleem and work on the railway in Leeds, laying down tracks. It's not clear if it was the heavy lifting, the working conditions, or the conversations with his colleagues (one imagines they weren't James Joyce or Hemingway fans)—but he lasted less than a week and emerged from the experience further committed to dedicating his life to literature.

I was born in the Maritimes of Canada. I wouldn't recognize the home I was born in if I were sitting in it right now, but I often imagine who and what I would have been if we had never left. Or if we had never gone there in the first place. I learned, just a few years ago, that Dad had received scholarships from two universities. One in New Brunswick, Canada, and one in New Jersey, USA. Some older, wayward uncle in the family had spent a year abroad in Montreal in the fifties and simply muttered, "Canada has nicer people." It's not clear if that man had even been to the US. But that line alone was enough to convince my parents to set their sights on New Brunswick. Since I heard that little tidbit, not a week has gone by where I don't wonder who I might have become if New Jersey had been a more tempting offer. I was already such a huge fan of Bruce Springsteen and Bon Jovi when I was growing up. I guess the old saying is true: you can't keep the Jersey out of the guy whose dad almost moved to Jersey.

In early 1970s New Brunswick, my father made friends with a man named Zia Doja. In those days, in that homogeneously white environment of the Canadian Maritimes, my parents were desperate to meet anyone of *any* ethnic background that might remind them even a little of home. My dad would tell me that any time they'd see an ethnic person, he and my mom would say to each other, *"Woh dekho, apna!"* (Look over there, one of ours!) Guyanese? *APNA!* Lebanese? *APNA!* White man with a good tan? *APNA!* And with that attitude in hand, my dad met tons of international students. Nigerians with whom he could talk about the writings of Chinua Achebe. West Indians with whom he could talk about the works of V. S. Naipaul. And Zia Doja, with whom he could talk about anything.

Zia Doja came from India, and given what you now know about India and Pakistan, thanks to the most succinct historical lesson of all time that I gave you earlier, it stood to reason that they would have a strong connection. And so, Zia became Uncle Zia. In the Brown world, every friend of your parents immediately becomes an uncle or aunty. In Zia's case, he *earned* the "Uncle."

My Italian friends get a kick out of the fact that I have an Uncle Zia. In Italian, *zio* is "uncle," and *zia* is "aunty." So I'm essentially calling this man "uncle-aunty." Which suggests some kind of transgender identity that wasn't in place. In reality, Uncle-Aunty was my father's consigliere, guiding Dad on a multitude of decisions throughout his life. At different times, Uncle Zia convinced my dad to get a VCR, a microwave, and a computer. Perhaps most important of all, he guided my father toward Montreal. Again, one comment or conversation, and the complete trajectory of a life, and lives to follow, is changed. It never ceases to amaze me. May you all have an Uncle Zia in your lives to help combat your own father's paralyzing fear of change.

Thanks to Uncle Zia's advice, both my parents tucked into long careers at Dawson College, a Montreal institution of higher learning. My mother got a job as a secretary, and my father as an English teacher. Dawson College, in the 1970s, was also a haven for free-thinking hippies, draft dodgers, and various weirdos who somehow became professors. These people turned out to be perfect colleagues, and teaching English turned out to be the ideal job for him.

In some families, the most important thing is making money. In others, it's religion. In my childhood home, it was grammar.

While my dad maintained a variety of "side hustles" throughout his life, first and foremost he was an English teacher. This was *great* for me because of all the incredibly interesting things I got to learn about sentence structure and syntax. For example, did you know that a gerund is a nonfinite verb form that has the properties of both verb and noun, such as being modifiable by an adverb and being able to take a direct object? Yeah, cool stuff like that. Yes, I'm being a bit of a jerk right now—realistically, I wouldn't have been able to write this book without Dad's constant critici—I mean, coaching—throughout my life. It *was* helpful, but at times a little restrictive. Double negatives were a "no-no," and you'd always need to plan how your sentences were going to end before they came out of your mouth.

"Dad, where's the turkey at?"

"No, no, no—you cannot end a sentence with a preposition."

"Dad, I just need some turkey to make a sandwich with!"

"You did it again!"

"Fine—*with which* to make a sandwich!"

"Better. I finished the turkey yesterday."

The other way to live with my dad's constant grammar rules was to have a sense of humour about them. "Father! Where doth said turkey lie? Might I procure for myself a breaded meal of some sort?"

Above and beyond grammar, education was truly important in our family. I come from a lineage that has always valued academia and higher learning. So high in fact, that even after I completed university, my dad never missed a chance to remind me, "You only have a bachelor's degree. A bachelor's degree is nothing!" *I know, Dad. I have one, and for the last two years I've been selling video equipment full-time at a place called Future Shop.*

As a person who eventually got an MBA and an IT degree, neither of which I use today, I can't say I wholeheartedly agree about the "value" of education.

I mentioned my father's side hustles: he taught Third World Fiction at Dawson College, English as a Second Language (ESL) at Concordia University, Urdu at McGill University, and was also a poet, a short story writer, and a translator for the government. His father was the principal of a school—a headmaster, as they say in the old country. My maternal uncle Shahryar was a poet, and his father, my maternal grandfather, was in fact a very famous and influential poet in Pakistan, considered to be the "father of modernism" in Urdu literature. And then there is me: a man who built his career on a foundation of fart jokes. High-quality fart jokes, mind you, not the pedestrian stuff. But fart jokes, nonetheless. I've lost count of how many of my grandfather's fans I have personally disappointed over the years at various events.

"Ah, so you are N. M. Rashed's grandson!"

"I am."

"It's so nice to meet you! Your grandfather was a great man! What are you doing here?"

"I'll be performing onstage in a few minutes, poking fun at the shape of kebabs and talking about cousins marrying each other."

They're typically gone seconds after this, muttering something about an erosion of culture.

What you grow up with affects you more than you realize, and it can come out in surprising ways. Once, when I was about thirteen years old, my friend and I were at another buddy's house. His parents were originally from India and were huge Bollywood fans. In those days, Bollywood movies came out on VHS cassettes that were dubbed over again and again until the quality of the tape was so bad you could barely read the name of the film in the opening credits. These days, the average new television will have a pixelization of over a million. On those VHS cassettes, you got a pixelization of about forty-five. You could count each pixel by hand. Be that as it may, one fine day at my friend's house we found ourselves a VHS cassette labelled with a number of Xs on it. That number was three. It was suspicious and required further investigation. Lo and behold, it was a dirty Bollywood movie. Something absolutely unheard of at the time. Our friend played it for about ten seconds, then gasped and immediately stopped it. He needed a minute to recover from the fact that his dad (and maybe mom) had rented this video, and we all needed a minute to come to terms with the fact that videos like this existed at all.

Bollywood at that time was hero and heroine dances in open fields, in lush mountain valleys, and around trees. And if and when two pairs of lips—after an excessively long, hyper-choreographed musical substitution for foreplay—were about to be pressed together, they would flash-cut to the next day, a scene wherein the couple might be seated at a breakfast table or in a temple, smiling shyly at each other. *Okay . . . but hello? WHAT THE HELL HAPPENED LAST NIGHT?* I was always left wondering. There was such a thing as leaving *too much* to the imagination, and eighties Bollywood was all about that.

And so, the filth we were watching on this random Saturday afternoon at the then tender age of thirteen was both surreal and mesmerizing. To be Brown and thirteen and living in the 1980s meant you firmly believed that no Brown woman had ever had sex. In this video, we watched a shapely woman— a boss's assistant, if we were to give her a title—walk into a disgustingly sweaty and round man's office. To be clear, the office was square, the man was round. She had a request of him. Her request could be granted, of course, but there would be conditions. The first of those conditions involved him putting her on his desk and heaving his now naked and hard-to-ignore body against her. We watched in jaw-dropping silence, in both horror and absolute bewilderment, hoping there wouldn't be any other conditions. Suddenly, the assistant spoke out: "It's paining. It's paining." At that point, almost instinctively, I grabbed the remote, pressed pause, and confidently said, "Come on! 'Paining' isn't a verb."

"Paining" isn't a verb. Wow. It was like the words *"Are you a f^%&ing idiot"* actually flew out my friends' eyes. They yelled at me, *"PRESS PLAY! This is the greatest moment of our lives!"* Oops, yes, sorry about that. Don't know what came over me! But I did know. It was my father's incessant grammar policing. To this day, I haven't quite been able to shake it. By "it" I mean the images in that video *and* the intolerance for bad grammar. If you describe something to me as being "more better," it really does take every bit of my strength to not say, "Ummm . . . It's just 'better.'" I don't want to say it, but at some level I need to. So, to everyone in my life, both past and future: I apologize.

Interestingly, while my dad was a very articulate man, he also had a real love for swearing. And yet, it was somehow the classiest swearing you'd ever hear: "These sons of bitches, for whom I have reserved only the highest of contempt . . ." My mom on the other hand had an obscenely clean mouth. I quite literally only heard her swear once in my entire life, and it didn't even really count. She was dealing with some unbearable administrative officer at her work—someone who thought very highly of herself and went out of her way to demean secretaries. My mom was absolutely fed up with this person and finally said, "That woman is a real . . . bitch . . . type . . . person." Aw, Mom, you were so close, but you just couldn't stick that landing, hey? There was no way my mother could allow "the b-word" to just stand out there on its own.

Education was a constant in the home. Islam, however, existed more on the periphery. It was present in the margins of the document of my life. I wasn't raised in a religious Muslim household, and I certainly didn't take on the opportunity (read: challenge) of practising on my own. Much like education, religion doesn't always make an impact when you're a kid.

Muslims, you may know, are required to pray five times a day. As a kid, I remember thinking, *Gosh, that's a lot of praying.* Now, as an adult in my late forties, I think, *Gosh, that's a lot of bending.* I would have been *so* much more flexible if I'd been observant.

We did have observant relatives who would come to visit. Inevitably, if you are a practising Muslim, your visit to someone's home will overlap with at least one prayer time. My father would always provide those guests with one of our mildly used prayer mats, point them toward Mecca (the direction in which you are supposed to pray), and then politely decline their offers to join them. It was Dad's twist on the old "After you? No, after *you* . . ." This was more "After you? No, *only* you."

One aspect of Islam that we did observe was Eid. It is a very important Muslim holiday. In essence, it's like Muslim Christmas. It's the biggest holiday of the year—but twice. We have two different Eids, but both times they are called the same thing. It's reminiscent of a time when the Canadian Football League had two teams that were both named the Roughriders (the entire league only consists of nine teams). Two different teams, in two completely different places in the country—same name. I remember occasionally thinking that Eid might do well with a sexy rebrand and that it needn't go down the Roughriders route (I was eight—I probably didn't use the words "sexy rebrand").

Eid was also the only time, as a young boy, that I would see my father pray: when we'd get in the car and biannually drive to a converted hockey arena for Eid prayers. Because my family had a habit of always being late—Mom and Dad each had this habit but blamed the other—we needed to go to the largest prayer gathering in the city to guarantee ourselves a spot, no matter what time we rolled in. The arena, on a side note, was called Paul Sauvé Arena, named after a former Québécois premier and leader of the right-wing Union Nationale party. The arena staged wrestling matches in the seventies, and Jimi Hendrix even played a concert there. I can't help but feel that members of this nationalistic party, while having no problem with men in their underwear throwing each other around or a Black man playing guitar high on LSD in their "leader's arena," would have drawn the line at Muslims praying to Allah.

During that car ride, my father would embarrassingly have to remind me of the prayers I'd need to do (embarrassing for both of us), and in that arena I'd wonder why it was so difficult for me to stay in a prayer position on my knees. Like, men in their nineties looked as if they'd been born in that position, whereas I was wincing five minutes into a one-hour sermon. This kneeling, butt to heel, is called the "hero position" in yoga, by the way. I know this, because when I couldn't do it in a yoga class and was made to feel like quite the non-hero, I made a mental note to hate yoga a little more.

The full story is that Eid al-Fitr is the festival to "break the fast," as it follows the month of Ramadan, the holy month in the Muslim lunar calendar in which Muslims fast from sunup to sundown for thirty days. Eid al-Adha is the festival to commemorate when the prophet Abraham—depending on your interpretation—either had a dream or received a command from God to sacrifice the eldest of his two sons (Ishmael) as a show of obedience to God. It's considered the holier Eid of the two, which, as the father of two sons, makes a lot of sense to me. FYI, for those of you on the edge of your seats about how this Abraham story ends: just before Abraham could sacrifice his son, God replaced the boy with a lamb to sacrifice instead. As you can imagine, Eid has become a time of great fear for lamb everywhere.

Lamb consumption notwithstanding, my practise of religion was perfunctory and performative. While I can't claim that was genetic, it did feel like something I inherited from my parents. My mother's connection to Islam was fairly private; she'd go pray in her room, occasionally, and not make a big deal of it at all. We'd barely know she was gone. And Dad only seemed to remember Islam during the holidays. I found out after his death that my father used to send money back to Pakistan every year, to a religious pir he once knew. A pir is a Sufi saint who guides and teaches disciples of Sufism, which is by far the most spiritual and mystical of any Muslim practise, so much so that many Muslims don't regard Sufis as followers of Islam at all. I guess my dad met this man on one of his trips to Pakistan and liked the cut of his jib. It also meant that my dad had a connection to Islam after all. But where did that leave me? And what could I possibly pass on from that to my own children?

Chapter 2

THE WONDER YEARS

MY CHILDREN DON'T HAVE any friends in our west Toronto neighbourhood, and it irks me. Sometimes my wife and I wonder, is it us? Are *we* the problem? Should she and I be friendlier? Should we be going door to door and introducing ourselves to other families, inviting parents with kids over for dinner or drinks? But that's ridiculous, right? When I was a kid, you walked out your front door and other kids were just *there*, ready to play. Our cups runnethed over with friends! No parent *ever* had to introduce their kid to you. If anything, the kids were the ones introducing their parents to each other!

My childhood street was a very cosmopolitan, secular block that included kids of many backgrounds. And while their ethnic heritage may have come up from time to time, I don't remember us talking about it much. And we never even *thought* about religion!

Well, that's not entirely true. *I* thought about religion—any time one of my friends was eating bacon. See, the one thing I knew for certain as a child, the one unwavering fact, was that the pig was a dirty animal and "*We don't eat pork.*" Furthermore, the suggestion was that if you *do* eat pork, you will go to hell. At a young age, I accepted this without question. But then I'd notice my white friends' reactions when their moms were making bacon. Their excitement was—well, let's just say it seemed like bacon was a gift from God himself.

No matter, at least us non-white kids would be together in this crusade against pork. But then my Black neighbour told me that his mother was frying bacon. On his face, too, there was nothing but joy. Oh well, at least us Brown kids were together in this loose crusade against pork. But then I saw my Brown friends—Hindus and Christians—enjoying bacon and I felt completely excluded from what seemed like a really fun activity. My friends were closing their eyes, taking bites of bacon, and then sighing deeply, as though they were being transported to another time and place. You're seven! Where could you be getting transported to? You've seen nothing!

Finally, I snapped:

> *Okay, fine! I don't eat bacon! I am a Muslim and I'm not allowed to eat bacon, so I don't! Even though allll my friends eat bacon. But I won't, because I want to go to heaven one day. But here's my question: Once I've lived this bacon-free existence for all my years, once I've made what seems like a pretty big sacrifice based on the general consensus among seven-year-olds, WILL THERE BE BACON FOR ME TO FINALLY TRY IN HEAVEN?*

There has to be, right? *Hello, Allah, are you there? It's me, Ali.* The silence and/ or frowns, depending on who I was asking, were unsettling. People were none too pleased with my question. And I was none too pleased with their silence.

In my sons' first school, they had *tons* of Muslim students, and therefore very little bacon temptation. Not only that, but once, a kid said to my son, "Don't share your lunch with *that* kid, he's a different kind of Muslim than us." *What the . . . ?* First of all, don't share your lunch with anyone. All kids are germy and disgusting. Secondly, your school is so Brown that you have the "privilege" of being able to discriminate against certain types of other Muslims? These kids have it so good.

For better or worse, my childhood—with only two and a half channels on television (PBS wouldn't really count as a channel until I was ten, and the box with the ABC/NBC/CBS trio was still a few years away), constant play of some kind happening outside, and a plethora of diverse friends—shaped me into who I would become.

———

24

When I moved to Montreal, I was three. I have no memory of the apartment my parents picked out. But I hear good things. It was in the east end of the city, just blocks away from Olympic Stadium. That area was a touristy dream of a location, the stadium itself was where the 1976 Montreal Olympics took place and, most important, it was the home of my beloved Montreal Expos baseball team. It would have been an Airbnb owner's wet dream, had Airbnb existed. For years afterward, I wondered what possessed my parents to move away from that primo spot. Eventually the Expos baseball team folded and pieces of concrete from Olympic Stadium were notoriously falling off and I stopped being nostalgic for a place I didn't even remember to begin with.

Two years later, my parents chose Brossard, Quebec, to settle down in. The municipality of Brossard is subdivided by letters. The A section, the B section. No C section back then, however. You might be thinking, "Oh, is that out of respect for women who have given birth via caesarean and don't need their neighbourhood to be a constant reminder of their possibly traumatic procedure?" No. Sadly, "respect for women" was never a top priority in this province. There was also no D, E, F, G, or H section, so who knows what logic was being applied. Our first foray into Brossard was the P section. I guess the possibility of residents having a constant reminder of urinating was no issue for the people who planned our neighbourhood.

Our street was all row townhouses with thin walls, and a general vibe that "this is cute, but we won't be staying very long." And to that point, not one of the families we knew there wound up staying for good. Our street in the P section was very clearly a launching pad; it was where twenty- and thirty-something adults—certainly the newer immigrants—would be getting their first jobs in the 1970s and '80s, saving some money, and then moving on to establish themselves elsewhere.

Although, when I say "saving money," as a responsibility to the truth I should state that my father excluded himself from that activity. Dad oscillated between middle class and "flat broke" every few weeks. He'd even turn his pockets inside out to illustrate it to us, as if "flat broke" didn't quite hammer home the point.

With his money or without it, from ages four to seven, I was blessed to meet a colourful array of friends—some of whom I would continue to be close to for the rest of my life. My parents moved from an almost homogeneously white city in New Brunswick, where yogurt was "ethnic food," to a municipality that later would hold the title of the most culturally diverse city in Canada. Our friends and neighbours included two Indian Hindu families, two white, anglophone families, a French-Irish family, a Vietnamese family, a Chinese family, a Nigerian family, and a Pakistani-American family.

Michael Haynes was my neighbour on one side. And beside him was a kid named Lawrence. They weren't members of culturally diverse communities, but they were minorities in their own right—anglophones in a French-speaking province. Stacy Burns was my neighbour on the other side—he was the product of an Irish dad and a French mother. His mother was my first introduction to perfect bilingualism, sometimes even in the same sentence: *Stacy, viens ici maintenant, your father wants to see you.* I remember marvelling at that, not in the least bit appreciating the fact that my mother was doing the exact same thing, just in Urdu and English, and sometimes Punjabi, too.

The rest of the street had an unusual cast of characters that included my friend Talib—who, as I alluded to above, had a Kentuckian mother, a Pakistani father, and a dog named Poochie, who quite literally bit a chunk out of my mom's butt. That's a memory that'll stay with both our families forever. One of my best friends was named Tonyefa. He would always appeal to his mother to call him "Tony" around all of us, but she was having none of it. From Tony I learned three things: first, where Nigeria was; second, that newly trained and immigrant doctors had to work in the most remote parts of Canada; and third, where the city of Gander, Newfoundland, was. That's right—courtesy of Tonyefa's dad's medical postings, I learned about Gander, long before 9/11 and the *Come from Away* Broadway show!

There were also two different pairs of Indian brother and sister siblings: Madhuri and Mangesh, and Manish and Bhavna. The latter remain my good friends to this day. The story goes that one day at the local grocery store, from her seated position in a grocery cart, a three-year-old Bhavna shouted out, "Look, Mummy, one of us!" when she saw my mother. The tables had turned, and Bhavna was pulling an *"Apna!"* on my parents. My mom and Aunty Amita (immediately an "aunty") established that they lived right near each other, and that chance grocery store meeting kick-started a lifelong friendship for me and for my parents.

Across the street from my house was a tiny crescent that had a grassy area the size of a baseball infield in its centre. That infield was pretty much where I lived. Not one of us ever picked up a phone to invite a friend to play. It was either knocks on doors, or just casual strolls to the field with a bat or ball or rock in hand, and neighbourhood kids would follow suit within minutes. We played soccer, football, tag, Marco Polo, a vague sport called Boys vs. Girls (the activity didn't matter as long as we were against each other), and a lot of Follow the Leader. Madhuri was always the leader for some reason. I hear she's a radiologist now, but man, her real skill was bossing around groups of dopey boys.

That grassy area is where I even fractured my shoulder during some kind of made-up baseball-soccer hybrid game. *Don't slide into home until you learn how to slide* was the lesson from that day. These were the days of one family television, in the one TV room. Our TV room, as luck would have it, looked right out onto the field. So, while I recovered for six weeks with a shoulder injury, I had to look out our bay window and see all my friends having the time of their lives. To people outside, I must have resembled a sad puppy wondering if his owner would ever come back.

I was also playing in that crescent the day that my baby sister came home. I remember my parents coming back from the hospital and calling me inside, saying, "Come meet your sister!" Naurooz was born three months premature, which was a hell of a big deal in 1977. She came into the world the size of a telephone receiver and had been kept in the NICU for months before being let out of the hospital. I ran inside thinking, *Okay, this is kind of cool—she's here!* About four minutes later, my thoughts flipped to *I hope I can get back to playing in the crescent soon.* The makings of a solid big brother, right there.

As I finished off the second grade, I remember most of my neighbourhood friends starting to move away. It turned out that we were not going to be an exception to this exodus. The Hassans had to shoot their shot as well.

———

Just as I was reaching the age of eight, we busted out of our townhouse in the P section. It was time. We had grown, we had evolved, we were moving on up—wait for it—to a bungalow in the S section of Brossard! Yes, that sounds very much like a lateral, risk-averse move on paper, but for us it was an improvement. It was a stand-alone house. We wouldn't hear our neighbours' conversations through paper-thin walls, and they wouldn't smell my dad's cigarettes through the vents. And from a classist perspective, the S section looked down their nose on the P section. We couldn't be rubbing elbows with new immigrants anymore—why, we had been in the country for more than *ten years*!

For me, the move meant a new neighbourhood, a new school, and new friends. The first friend I made—and still a dear friend today—was Zach Moos. I met Zach on the first day of third grade. My new school was called St. Lawrence Elementary, named after the mostly frozen, entirely polluted, generally un-swimmable St. Lawrence River. We were all queued up to go into school that morning and from about ten feet behind me, Zach called out, "Ali!" I was surprised that anyone knew me at this new school, but I responded with a "Yeah?" Zach looked me over and made his introduction: "Who the hell are you?" Well, wasn't that just the makings of a lasting friendship. It turns out there was another Ali in this school.

Zach was Parsi and spent most of our youth pleading, "There's no *e* at the end of 'Moos'!" Being Parsi might mean something to you, as it was recently popularized in the movie *Bohemian Rhapsody* as the ethnic background of Queen's frontman, Freddie Mercury. Freddie was always Parsi, it just took a movie for the world at large to find out. Parsis are a community that were originally from Pars, aka Persia, who practised the religion of Zoroastrianism, but who resettled in various parts of world, particularly in India. They were actually run out of Persia because of their religious beliefs, by the Muslim community there—as Zach never failed to remind me.

Despite our feuding ancestors, I was always welcome in Zach's home and fed like a king. Mrs. Moos was an avid baker who always had a cake sitting on a platter on the island of their kitchen. She also made incredible meat loaf and curries and pies. (Full disclosure, Mr. Moos was also the first man I know who got gout, so eating like a king does have its consequences.) Her food was so good that one time when a glass casserole dish of her lasagna cracked in the oven, Mr. Moos, in an abundance of caution, threw out the entire casserole so none of us might eat glass by accident. As that lasagna slid slowly out of the dish and into their trash can, I remember holding myself back from yelling, *No! I'll eat it carefully! If I die, so be it. People will say, "He died doing what he loved: eating Mrs. Moos's food!"*

Another one of my close friends was Tom, who was South Indian, specifically Malayali. Just to give you an idea of how sweet Tom's family was, Zach and I once asked him to tell us a dirty word in Malayalam, his parents' language. He thought long and hard and finally came up with "Oh yeah— *muttattala!*" We were a little confused about how long it took him to remember this dirty word, but more confused to find out it meant "egghead"!

What? We just told you the most horrendous words in Punjabi and Gujarati involving mothers and their genitals, and you're giving us "egghead"? "Well, I don't know . . . It's the only swear word my dad has ever used!" Anecdotally, the suggestion is that many non-native English speakers turn to their native tongue when they are beyond furious, for the comfort of those uniquely powerful swear words they grew up with. If "egghead" is as bad as it got, this family lived a good life!

Growing up with all of these cultures together was, I believe, good for all of us. We got exposed to different languages and traditions, different religions and customs, and, most important for me, I got to sample amazing foods from all over the world. But kids can be . . . how to put this . . . morons. Let's say that the learning curve for tolerance and acceptance of other cultures was pretty steep.

I've been asked many times if I've ever faced racism. I have, but jeez, it's so hard to pick a favourite. The list is fairly long, and no one's trying to write *A Suitable Boy* here. So, let's just focus on some "highlights," if you will.

Grade three or four, it must have been. I remember we were playing this annoying game (as kids often do), going around in a circle and asking, "Where were *you* born?" There were five kids, and my friend Scott went first: "I was born in Montreal, at the Royal Victoria Hospital." A Chinese kid went next and said he was born in Ottawa. I remember thinking that might be a lie because he did have a significant Chinese accent. Then it was my turn—happy with how unique I was going to sound, I proudly told everyone I was born in Fredericton, New Brunswick. I remember a pause as these kids tried to process what that could possibly mean to them. Scott burst out: "New Brunswick? You're a Newfie, you're a Newfie!" And they all laughed.

You know what—if that *is* racism, I guess it was not actually directed at me? If anything, this might have been a case of mistaken identity. With some ignorance of Canadian geography thrown in for good measure. Either way, it didn't feel good to be laughed at, and I was pretty bummed about it. Bummed enough that my father even noticed.

"What's the matter with you?"
"They called me a Newfie at school, Dad."
"Newfie? Ha hah! You're not a Newfie, you're a Pakistani!"

Empowered by this knowledge and encouraged by that supportive tone, I went back to school the next day and announced to my inner circle, "By the *way* guys, I'm not a Newfie, I'm a Pakistani!"

And, plot twist, cue the racism!

Another time, in grade five, it was definitely not a case of mistaken identity. A kid named Jonathan called my friend Zach and me "Pakis." I can't remember if it was Zach or myself, but one of us responded, "Yeah, well, you're a Limey!" We might as well have said "dum-dum head." *I'll see your ethnic slur, and I'll raise you a "dodo bird"! Does that sting? DOES IT?*

Of course it didn't—it was a useless retort. And it bothered me from that day on that there was no response to a white kid calling me a Paki. "Honky"? That just reminds me of a fun old-timey horn noise. "Cracker"? They're delicious on their own and taste even better with other white-coloured things on them, like cheese, butter, or sour cream dip. Dammit, whitey, you've rigged the system!

There really was no good response to that insult. Worse still, the next time we Brown kids were surrounded and called Pakis, Tom responded with "*I'm* Indian!" and then pointed at me. "*He's* the Pakistani!" Sigh. A few things to parse out there.

1. I thought we were in this together, Tom, you bastard.
2. This eleven-year-old probably doesn't care for his racism to be corrected. He would have called a pair of Mexicans "Pakis."
3. Pakistan *was* India not so long ago, Tom. Why don't you tell them that!

Despite all that (or maybe because of it, who knows?), Zach and Tom were my closest Brown friends, and Lee and Jeff were my closest white friends. When I say Lee was white, I mean white as in the don't-give-him-a-friendly-slap-on-the-back-on-Monday-morning-because-for-*sure*-he-sunburned-his-shoulders-at-the-cottage-on-the-weekend type of white. Lee joined our group of friends a little late, because his family had been living in Saudi Arabia of all places!

That's right: the first person I met who had lived in Saudi Arabia was a white, often sunburnt kid named Lee. His father had worked there when Lee was in elementary school, so Lee had actually grown up in what was called a "compound," in Jeddah, for a few years. And, interestingly, his connection to Islam was on par with mine at the time.

As we got older, Jeff and I connected on music, above all else. Glam rock, in particular. Bands like Poison, Mötley Crüe, and Guns N' Roses. Inspired by all these musicians we loved, our high school fashion sense was primarily composed of jeans, leather, and bandanas. Lots of bandanas. It was a strange time.

Unlike our old place in the P section, our home in the S section was neatly decorated—my mom had no tolerance for mess. The old house had beautiful Pakistani art and artifacts, but seemed less organized. Once we moved, my mother must have made it clear to my dad that the S in "S section" did *not* stand for smoking. So, it had to happen outside, and at my father's office. I was told years later that his friend and teaching colleague Enrique asked to be transferred out of their shared office because my dad smoked too much. And Enrique was also a smoker! I remember my friend Zach would stay over at my place, and we'd both be awoken in the basement by my dad's aggressive coughing, hacking, and spitting up God knows what, aka his "morning ritual." Zach asked me once, seemingly afraid to know the answer, "Is your dad okay?" That was the first indication I ever got that other dads weren't doing this every morning. By the time I was eighteen, he had angina and smoking became a thing of the past.

In our S section bungalow, our basement was split in half. One half was our television room. It was in that room that I perfected Nintendo's *Super Mario Bros.*, while ignoring my mother's screams for me to come eat supper already before she tossed the video game into the garbage. It was also in that room that I watched hours and hours of *This Week in Baseball*, WWF wrestling (while ignoring slanderous heckles from my father that "it's all fake!"), and PBS cooking shows. It was also on those bare wooden floors where I (unsuccessfully) practised my head spin, back spin, windmill, and many other never-quite-perfected break-dancing moves. On a related note, I almost died in that basement at least three times. I have a weak neck, I learned, midway through more than a few act-outs from the movie *Breakin' 2: Electric Boogaloo*.

The other half of the basement was my father's sanctuary. And by "sanctuary" I mean it was the battleground where my mother's minimalism fought against my father's hoarding. Mom ran a pretty tight ship and the only place my father could really do what he wanted was in the one and a half rooms he had in the basement. His library consisted of over ten thousand books, and packages of additional books arrived at our door on a monthly basis. Dad would greet the delivery guy with an "Ah, good. Finally!" which stood in stark contrast to my mom's "Oh God, what is *this* now?!" I remember more than a few deliverymen standing at our door, analyzing the vastly contrasting energies in the house, and looking like they needed to get the hell out of there.

Also in his office, my dad had three desks. One on which he read and wrote, one on which he shoved books that could no longer fit on the shelves, and one that housed his typewriter, wherefrom the word "DAMN!" would often be heard, followed by a waft of liquid paper. Depending on your age, you might need to take a few minutes now to do an internet search on "typewriter" and "liquid paper." My children, certainly, have no idea what they are. I have tried to explain what typewriters are to each of them and it's just too much for them to absorb. "But how did you save your files? How did it work if you didn't have to plug it in? So there was no delete key?!"

Unlike my dad's sprawling basement mess, my bedroom was an actual sanctuary, and there was nothing that could disturb it, except for my mother. Any time I slept in past 9 a.m. on a summer's day or even a weekend, my mother would barge in, yelling that I'd "wasted half the day!" Again, we were not farmers, and have never in our ancestry been farmers, so that math doesn't work at any level.

My mother's overbearing presence notwithstanding, I regarded my bedroom as a shrine. A temple, if you will. A temple where one might pray to the gods of rock and roll and heavy metal. And the roots of that must be credited to a Pakistani family friend named Nadeem Janjua. The first time our family visited his small apartment, I remember this long-haired, brooding Brown teen nodding me over to his bedroom. He leaned back in a chair, I sat on his bed, and our first conversation went like this:

Nadeem: You know *Kiss*?
    Me: (*Hoping he meant the band.*) I've heard of them.
Nadeem: (*Eye roll.*) You should know Kiss. You know Ozzy?
    Me: I know some Ozzy.
Nadeem: (*Sigh.*) You heard of Randy Rhoads?
    Me: I think so?
Nadeem: No. You should *know* Randy Rhoads.

He then proceeded to test my knowledge of heavy metal by playing me song after song on his guitar. Van Halen. Followed by Black Sabbath. Followed by Iron Maiden. Followed by Judas Priest. "You know this one? What about this one?" My knowledge was deemed to be incomplete and unsatisfactory, and he gave me homework to do "for next time." A fifteen-year-old cool-as-hell guitar virtuoso was guiding me through the annals of heavy metal. And he was Pakistani! He was four years older than me, and at that age it was a hugely significant age gap. He was in high school; I was in elementary school. Fifteen-year-olds didn't talk to eleven-year-olds, sometimes not even when they're siblings!

As a parent, you worry about who your kids meet. They could influence them to do drugs. Or engage in crime. Or in my case, grow a mullet. Nadeem eventually had to move on to friends his own age, but his legacy lived on in my bedroom, in the form of hundreds of magazine pages and posters that lined my walls. At one point, when I was about fifteen, I'm pretty sure every single square inch of white wall had been covered with posters of lead singers, drummers, and guitarists. I was forced to expand to the ceiling—an Iron Maiden flag featuring "Eddie" greeted me each morning overhead. Every poster was music-related, with maybe two or three posters of cars. I don't actually remember any posters of cars, but I'm throwing it in there to deflect from the idea that my teens were spent staring exclusively at men in tight leather pants and spandex. And when I say "tight," I mean you could actually *see* that David Lee Roth was Jewish in a couple of those posters.

As I reflect upon that time, I find it interesting that not one of my friends ever came over, looked at the walls, and said, "Okay . . . this is a little . . . gay." And yet, in my twenties and thirties, any time I wore a pink shirt ("It's salmon, dammit!"), I didn't have to wait three minutes for someone to gleefully bark, "Nice shirt, ya queer!"

Altogether, it was a pretty great way to grow up. I had a wide array of friends, and we all hung out together equally. But if I had to name the dominant culture, we were simply suburban Montreal kids. We played hockey, listened to similar music—and so what if some of us got better food at home? It all made sense and it fit. Between the family friends, neighbourhood friends, and strangers we'd meet, the general consensus was that our world was overall a diverse and accepting place.

As I look at my children and our neighbourhood now, I have to wonder—will my children have similar experiences? Clearly, growing up in a diverse community came with some baggage, but overall, the pros outweighed the cons.

An exposure to different people, customs, and backgrounds might just be the key to helping you grow up as a balanced (read: non-racist) person. Get out there, kids. Get to know other people and let them get to know you, too!

Chapter 3

A ROSE BY ANY OTHER NAME

IN 2010, I GOT MARRIED. Within a few months of me becoming a husband and new father to two young girls, we got another surprise. I suppose the classically Canadian way to describe the situation is to say that "I snapped one past the goalie." But really, my wife and I had discussed the possibility of having another child and figured we'd just see how it went.

The proverbial goalie had been pulled, shots were being fired willy-nilly, and no one was keeping score. Two months into our marriage, my wife delivered the absolutely stunning news that she was pregnant. I call it stunning because I'd long lost all faith that my sperm still had any "get up and go." After many years of a disciplined Québécois regime of cigarettes, booze, and long car rides with poutine tucked between my thighs, I just figured my baby-making ship had sailed.

We found out that the child was going to be a boy, and I quickly found myself in the stressful position of trying to find a suitable name for this kid. HOT TIP: Never tell relatives what you're thinking of naming your child! Well, never tell my relatives, anyway.

White men, generally, have it pretty easy. Rob. Will. David. Short, simple names with no follow-up questions. You rarely find someone intrigued by the name Chris and asking about its meaning. And if they were to ask, they'd likely hear something like "I think it was my grandfather's name. And it's a name from the Bible or something."

Inspired by this simplicity, but still keen to insert some level of ethnicity into his name, I made the error of pitching names to my dad.

Me: We are thinking about a simple Muslim name. Like Omar or Riyaz.

Dad: I knew an Omar in tenth grade. He was a real bastard. And Riyaz is a man's name, not a child's name.

Me: Okay . . . Also thinking about Pasha.

Dad: Pasha isn't a name. It's a title.

Me: All right, but we know three different Pashas and they all go by the "name" Pasha. So it's kind of a name, no?

Dad: What other names do you have in mind?

Me: Hmm . . . Maybe you should tell me what names *you* have in mind, Dad.

He did have some in mind. Oh, did he ever. My dad drafted up a list of the most poetic, yes, but also complicated names you'll have heard, even if you are Pakistani (apologies to people with these names): As-Sabur (The Patient One), Talib-e-Deedar (Seeker of Sight), and Shujaa'at (Bravery). How was this man, who had immigrated to Canada in the late sixties and immersed himself into all the best that the country had to offer, now coming up with the most ethnic suggestions of all time?

As strange as Dad's list was, it prompted a real "hold my beer" moment for my mom ("hold my chai," to be accurate). Three days before my son was due to be born, she called and told me, her voice full of excitement, "When you get home, check your email!" I could have told her I don't need to go home to check email anymore, but that wasn't important. I took the moment to tell my wife that there was another suggestion waiting in my in-box. We opened the email, and there it was: FAKHAR.

A real Pakistani name, to be sure, but just a supremely bad idea. A return phone call was in order.

"Mom? Do you not want my son to experience happiness?"

"Why? Oh . . . Oh, because the name sounds like *that* word?"

"Yes. That's going to be an issue."

"But it's pronounced 'fakh-hher.'"

"That doesn't help anything."

"Well, I mean, he can just explain to the other boys—"

"He's gonna be LONG DEAD BEFORE THAT OPPORTUNITY
PRESENTS ITSELF!"

I was flabbergasted. Explain to the other boys? Mom, have you even *been* to a playground? Are you familiar with schools? I almost got a beating for saying I was born in New Brunswick! A "Fakhar" isn't even getting a half minute to explain himself! *Ah yes, hello fellow classmates. I suppose you're all very curious about the origins of my name. Well, gather 'round, and I shall regale you with a tale of this interesting and exotic name that you must certainly be quite jealous of— Ahh . . . AHHHH! OOOWWW! Or, yes, I suppose you could instead just give me a wedgie and leave me hanging from a tree branch by my underwear.*

Arabic and Muslim names often have grandiose meanings behind them. For example, Sana is a female name which means "resplendence or brilliance." Azhar means "flower, blossoms, and the most shining or luminous." Afnan is a name meaning "full spreading branches of trees, growth, and fruitfulness." And it's potentially embarrassing, too, because you wouldn't be too keen to explain that your name means "the illumination the angels provide for your ascent to heaven" as you work the graveyard shift at a local burger joint.

For us, there were a lot of competing factors at work. The name should be simple, Muslim or ethnic-sounding, and not overly complicated in meaning. Inspired in part by my friend and comedian Maz Jobrani, and by the general simplicity and multicultural background of the name, we chose the name "Maaz." It means, quite simply, "brave." Presently, he scares pretty easily, but we're hoping he grows into the name eventually.

The takeaway from this entire naming exercise for me was that your name can shape your identity and your entire life. It can bring you joy or constant stress. In North America, a Chris is likely to have an easier go than, say, an Arsalaan. I use the name Arsalaan as an example because I have a dear friend with that name. And twenty-five years later, it still pains me to recall him trying to introduce himself to women in loud nightclubs.

"Wait, what's your name?"
"Arsalaan!"
"Epsilon?"
"Arsalaan!"
"Hair salon?"
"Ar-sa-laan."
"Slowing it down doesn't help!"
"Never mind. I'm gonna dance alone."
"Dance-a-long?"
"NEVER MIND!"

It might also amaze you to know how many ways there are to pronounce the three-letter name that is Ali.

My first exposure to the name would have been from my parents' mouths, and so the Pakistani pronunciation. The way my parents and family friends pronounce Ali starts with the *A* sound, like in "unforgiving." Yes, I know there's no *a* in unforgiving, that's where the confusion starts. And you end almost immediately, with a quick "li" as in "lee." "Uh-li," basically. Unless you're trying to convince me to do something I don't want to do, or are very disappointed in me, and then it's *Uh-leeeee*. Many people have taken to asking me, "How do you *actually* pronounce your name? Like, how would your mother pronounce it?" As well-intentioned as that is, dude, I don't want you, white person from the Niagara Region of Ontario, calling out my name like my mom does. That's weird. Also, when I hear "Uh-lee!" I think I'm in trouble or got caught doing something wrong, so let's try to keep that to an absolute minimum.

I also learned, at an early age, that there is a "true" pronunciation of the name Ali, held dearly by my friends and strangers who hail from the Middle East. Here's the best way I can describe this one: You start with an *a*, like you'd find in the word "apple." For a split second, it sounds like everything's going to be perfectly smooth and manageable, but then you have to very quickly transition into a guttural *a* that lives simultaneously in your Adam's apple *and* the back of your throat, like, "Aggkhhh," and then follow it up with a very short "li." Very short, because who has the energy for anything after a guttural *a*. Basically, "Aggkhhhli." It took me years to wrap my head around it. Many Arabs have chastised me, asking, "Why do you *bronounce* your name like 'Ali'? It is 'Aggkhhhli!'" I know it is, brother, but I don't enjoy dry-heaving when I'm introducing myself.

And by the way, if you're reading this book and mouthing out any of the above in a public place like a bus or a library, and you look like a cat trying to quietly expel a hair ball, I apologize.

For Canadians, my name was a combination of "alley," "a-LEE," "hah-lee"—which was more Quebec specific—or "AU-lee"—which really should be reserved for the Olivers in your life. Add to this the fact that I've happily been "Al" to well over half my friends for most of my life.

And "Hassan" is another beast. The Muslim pronunciation would be like the HUS in hustler, followed by a quick and abrupt N sound: Hussn. But most non-Brown people have called me either "HASS-in" or "hah-SAN" (as in sand) my entire life. So, like, who the hell am I, exactly?

I'm the Kristin of the Muslim world. Is it Krystin? Kurstyn? Kristeen? Kursteen? Keerstyn? Who knows? Every day brings a new option. The difference has always been that unlike every Kristin I've ever met, I don't *really* care. I know, that doesn't sit well with many people.

I once had the opportunity to interview Hasan Minhaj. If you don't know him, he's a Muslim American comedian and was the host of his own late-night-style talk show called *Patriot Act*. He has a famous story about how, on *The Ellen DeGeneres Show*, he walked Ellen back through his introduction and taught her how to say his name correctly. She had pronounced it "Ha-saaan Minhaaaj" and he informed her that it was in fact the "Hussn" I mentioned above, followed by a non-drawn-out Min-haj. He told me that his parents were in the live audience that day, and his father told him on their way home that he was absolutely mortified that his son would waste Ellen DeGeneres's time, on national television, to go through something as trivial as his name. Hasan's point to me was "I did it precisely because it *is* important. Ali, you know it is."

My response, though, was "Man, I'm not so sure it is."

The truth is, I don't connect with Uh-li Hussn any more or less than I connect with Ali Hassan.

In Canadian Punjabi families who immigrated here in the seventies, you'll sometimes see a series of siblings from oldest to youngest: Gary, Peter, Bob, Karen, and then Hansvinderpal. By the time the youngest came along, everyone had stopped pandering to the locals. So, all this begs the question, why would I connect with Gary over Hansvinderpal? Why do I, Canadian-born-and-bred Ali Hassan, side more with Indian-born immigrant to the United States Najme Minhaj than I do with his son, American-born and American-bred Hasan Minhaj?

The thing that I've never been able to fully comprehend is that my dad was Mr. Hah-saan or Professor Hah-saan his whole life. My mom was also Mrs. Hah-saan, to every non-Muslim she ever met. I have no memory of either of them ever correcting anyone. But any time a friend of mine would call and ask for "Al," my mother would mockingly answer the phone and say, "It's for ALLLLL." And stranger than that, she would correct my Muslim friends' names. When I met an Amreen—who we all called AM-reen—my mother jumped to her "defence" to say, "What is this 'AM-reen'? It's 'UMB-reen.'" Listen, Mom, I don't know what to tell you, but you're adding letters where they don't belong. She called herself AM-reen, so we call her that, too.

I went to elementary school with two kids named Farhan. That might be two more than you've ever met, but I guess the stars aligned for St. Lawrence Elementary School and we were blessed with a pair. They were both older than me, but I knew for a fact that they both pronounced their names "FAR-HAN." That's *Far*, as in "a galaxy far, far away," and *han* as in the first three letters of the word "hand." I used to spend some time with one of them in particular, playing a lot of street hockey. But any time I would say, "I was playing hockey with FAR-HAN" or "FAR-HAN was shoved into a locker today," my mother would immediately correct me. "Why do you call him 'FAR-HAN'? You should let these boys know it's 'fur-haaaaun.'" (That's "fur" as in your coat, and "han" as in "Han Solo.") Really, Mom? This guy is doing his damnedest to fit in, and I'm supposed to go to school and say, "Hey, man, you're pronouncing your name wrong. Everyone, gather 'round. He's saying it wrong! My mom told me."

Had I even tried to expose Farhan, I imagine he would have grabbed me by the shoulders and said, "Hey, I'm two letters away from sounding like a Fart in a Hand and no one has picked up on that, so why don't you shut the hell up and I'll try not to bring up the fact that you have the word ASS in *your* last name!" Hey, hey—we cool, baby. We cool. Given the fickleness of bullies in those days, they could have easily changed gears, looked at me and said, "Let's beat this idiot up, he sounds like a bigger loser than FAR-HAN."

In the eighties, on the South Shore of Montreal, there wasn't a Brown soul who was going to tell any of us that we were acting white or selling out (with the exception of my mom, but her entire approach was suspect). Our primary goal was to not get beat up.

As you get older you find other ways to protect yourself. Often, people in minority groups will change their speech or behaviour so they can better fit in. It's a decades-old phenomenon—a fairly serious one—called code-switching. In recent years it has received a lot of attention.

When it happens because the person feels they *need* to do it, it does far more harm than good. It creates a tension between self-expression and social acceptance. As in, who I am isn't good enough for the rest of you. It's a phenomenon that negatively impacts the Black community more than any other.

Any time any minority associates making changes with compliance to white people's expectations, it normalizes systemic racism. And, on the flip side, downplaying your own ethnicity or background can generate hostility from within your own group, where you can be accused of "acting white." Code-switching can be deemed necessary for the interests of professional advancement, social acceptance, or—as it pertained to us in our youth—just not getting a wedgie. For the guy who didn't even know how to pronounce his own name, switching, camouflaging, and trying to blend in came easy.

With all this background, you might wonder why I didn't just name my son "Mike" and make things as simple as possible. I'll tell you why.

In my first week of college, I was auditioning to be a "campus" DJ. The auditions were held in the same studio and for the same audience that you would play to if you got the job—the one hundred or so students inside a common space called the Band Ring. There was no AM or FM station broadcast; this room was the entire audience. I sat down and got the album I was going to play cued up. The station manager gave me a nod—I was up. I got on the mic and said, "Hey, my name is Ali. Or Uhli. But you can call me whatever you like." Even as I heard myself say the words, I thought, *Well, that might backfire.* And get this, it did. Before I could say anything more, one dude with great comedic timing was already yelling, "All right, Señor Dipshit!" loud enough for it to penetrate through the poorly soundproofed DJ booth. The truth is, I don't even remember which precise words he chose—it had to be some combination of *dumbass*, *immigrant*, and *queer*. The insults du jour, if you will. It was hurtful enough that even the girl sitting beside the guy punched his arm and he responded with a grimace, yelling, "What! The guy said call him anything!" I don't remember the words exactly, but I remember the feeling and the lesson. Commit to your name. And so, I committed to the very Canadian "alley" for Ali—my imperfect solution for different people from different backgrounds having a different pronunciation for my name.

And so, Maaz is Maaz because I wanted him to be a kid of Muslim Pakistani derivation with a somewhat Muslim Pakistani name, but also a name that only had one pronunciation. I would like to believe we saved him some time in the grand scheme of things—a few days total saved over a lifetime perhaps, where he doesn't have to explain, "Actually, it's pronounced . . ."

Now, technically—and you didn't hear it from me—Maz and Maaz are two different names with different pronunciations. That double *aa* in Maaz is a guttural *a*. It'll rarely, if ever, come up. But if my son decides to be the guy who walks people back to correct them with an "Actually, it's 'Ma'aagghhhzz,'" or, if he wants to go "full" assimilation—even more than his father did—and someday just become a Mike, well, that's on him.

Part 2

RELIGION

Chapter 4

SUNDAY SCHOOL

SCARBOROUGH IS A SUBURB OF TORONTO—a richly diverse area where you can have a Filipino fish and rice plate for breakfast, a Caribbean lunch buffet, and a shawarma platter for dinner, all within a four-block radius.

Scarborough, in 2011, was also the place where a particular progressive Islamic Sunday school resided. Sending our daughters to Islamic Sunday school felt like a good idea. Given that my wife and I had both attended one as children, it seemed like the best place for our young girls to learn about religion, now that it wasn't being taught in school. I learned about religions in school, my wife did, too, but none of my kids do now. The progressive element was important, too, because we didn't need our girls to come back and judge us. When my friend Aslam recommended this school, my wife and I were receptive.

But we found out that Scarborough was a thirty-minute drive from our house, and there ended the discussion of sending our daughters to Sunday school. Even the promise of fantastic cuisine at the end of the trip wasn't enough to entice us. It's probably for the best. Honestly, my main rationale for sending them to Sunday school was "If I had to suffer through it, they should have to suffer through it!"

When I was very young, my mother made it clear to me that I would be going to Islamic Sunday school. The arrangement was apparently non-negotiable. Mom had entered some kind of unbreakable contract with God, and I would be the "beneficiary."

An innocent victim in this agreement, I began attending Islamic Sunday school at the age of five—part of the original crew of a new Muslim Sunday school system that started in our neighbourhood in the late seventies. Ten years later, in my mid-teens, I was still in this school, experiencing the opposite of progress.

My friends from that time know that I had what one could best describe as an "Islamic block," akin to writer's block. Everything I was taught each Sunday was wiped from my mental hard drive by the next Sunday. Hard reset. Some people just can't learn French. Their minds don't work that way. Some are just terrible at math. We all know these people. And others—me—have some kind of block when it comes to religious education. And chemistry. And physics. Computer science. Statistics, too, if I'm listing them all.

Our Sunday school was called "Arabic school," which was a misnomer if there ever was one. The goal was to ensure that each kid finished the Quran. You finish the holy book, and you move on and make room for the next group of kids. To "graduate," we all had to read it in Arabic, *but* we were never taught to understand Arabic. So, we read hundreds and hundreds of pages of a book in a language we never understood. Pretty big oversight there, in my opinion, which continues to this day.

In my particular case, a laggard, lackadaisical reading pace meant I wasn't finishing the book, and so I wasn't graduating. All my friends moved on years before me. At fifteen, I was left behind, sitting beside ten- and eleven-year-olds. Can you visualize that? It's a *big* difference. It's basically me, at the six-foot frame I'm at right now, sitting among prepubescent children. This made for some poor self-esteem, and the result was that I had become deeply unmotivated. Every time I was called upon by the teacher, I had nothing of value to contribute.

Teacher: Ali, the five pillars of Islam are . . . ?
Me: I . . . I can't remember . . .
Teacher: Faith, Prayer . . . Ali?
Me: Seriously . . . I don't—
Teacher: Charity, and . . . Ali?

Me: Umm . . . Samosas?
Teacher: What!
Me: I don't know. Why do you ask me? You know I don't
have the answer. I never have the answer!

The five pillars, since we're on the subject, are the articles of faith, prayer (five times a day), charity, fasting in the month of Ramadan, and hajj (making a pilgrimage to Mecca). Sure, I know them all now, because there's no pressure on me to answer and the internet exists. When the teacher saw me struggling to remember the pillars, I could literally *feel* him holding back the words "You idiot, you've been coming here *for ten years*!" And he was right to be frustrated, because not only had it been ten years, but I had attended *every single Sunday* that the school was open for all of those ten years. Worst performance, best attendance—that was me. Although, it needs to be said that I tried to do everything in my power to derail this hot streak.

Jason Bateman said in an interview once that acting is basically this: When you were young, and you took a cookie from the jar, and your mother said, "DID YOU TAKE A COOKIE?" and you said, "No! Mom! I didn't. I swear," and you got away with it? Simply put, *that's* what good acting is.

Well, every weekend as a kid, I exited my bedroom and delivered a monologue of Oscar-worthy contention, in the interest of getting out of Sunday school. I really think that my acting skills were unparalleled at the time. And the thought of going to *any* Sunday school did actually make me a little sick, so in essence I was doing some early method work. Honestly, those performances rival anything I've done to this date. I was *deep* in character. I was picking up buzzwords throughout the week and using them to the best of my abilities.

"Mom, [*cough, cough*] Mom. I hate to say this, but I don't think I can go. My throat is so raw, if you just look at my mouth. I'm pretty sure I have salmonella in my [*pointing at neck*] uterus. Mom, please, it's not about me, I just don't want the other kids to get sick!"

She wasn't having it. She was never having it. Diarrhea! Malaria!

Gonorrhea! Nothing could crack this woman. In retrospect, maybe it wasn't the acting. I'm beginning to think that perhaps the script had its fair share of flaws.

There were other issues weighing on me as a young man in Sunday school. I don't think anyone was describing me as a feminist at the time, but I can wholeheartedly say I just didn't like the way young women were treated in the school. Because Muslims pray five times a day, half a day spent at Sunday school would coincide with at least one if not two of the prayer times. The women were always at the back. Why! I couldn't come to terms with it. (That was just the beginning. I've been in mosques where women prayed in what could only truly be described, if I'm being honest, as lattice-covered cages.) Why not side by side? Or, my teenaged brain reasoned, why can't the men be at the back from time to time? Would it be so bad for me to check out some of the teen girls that I was developing ridiculously uncomfortable crushes on?

The treatment of students by some of the teachers didn't help my enthusiasm about Sunday school, either. I remember a teacher yelling at a girl for writing with her left hand. *The left hand is the devil's hand!*" Is it? Is that how it goes?

"You know, apparently—and you didn't hear this from me—but she's living on the streets, engaging in petty crime to support a heroin habit."
"Yes, well. Makes sense. She *is* left-handed."

The imam/principal/teacher (he played a lot of roles), I learned, was not averse to some light corporal punishment if we stayed out at recess for a minute longer than we were supposed to. I remember my friend Naveed and I once decided that we weren't going to go back into school after lunch. It was our act of rebellion. We were just going to remain in the parking lot/asphalt play area and kick rocks to each other. The imam shouted out at us twice. Then we got a "Don't make me come over there," or some such equivalent. And then he made the long walk "over there" to come and get us. He grabbed us both by the ears and dragged us back inside the school. It ranks as one of the least inspirational acts of rebellion I've ever committed. On the bright side, I can still to this day remember the sound of something resembling a bone cracking inside my ear when he grabbed me, so no one can take that little memento away from me.

The lore was that this particular imam was the father of a certain Yasmeen Ghauri. She went on to be a supermodel. Look her up—she was something special, the product of a German-Pakistani marriage. Conveniently, we Pakistani boys ignored her German side completely and claimed her as all *"APNA!"* She was a source of huge pride, as though her $100,000 struts down the catwalk yielded us some tangible benefit. I guess it's no different from being a sports fan. "We did it!" Nah, we didn't do anything, pal. Twenty-five well-honed, incredibly disciplined athletes did something. But definitely, let's finish these chicken wings and act like their win directly changes the course of our lives.

All that to say, any time my ear is touched, I think of a supermodel from the early 2000s. This isn't the way my wife should find this out, but there you have it.

One very strange lasting legacy of those ten years is I'm always a little uncomfortable around bearded hipsters. Because they look exactly like the imams who taught us at Sunday school! Every time I see a hipster, I play a game: Imam or Hipster? Or radicalized white man? You can't be too careful these days. But, of course, there's an easy way to figure it all out. I just say: *"Assalamu alaikum?"* And if they say, "What?" then it's just a quick backpedal on my part: "Oh, sorry, never mind—I thought you were someone else. Cool, cool. Anyway, can I get a Labatt 50 and a glass of pickled eggs? Or whatever artisanal, handcrafted, bespoke product is on offer in your place of business?"

Fortunately for me, my Sunday school nightmare came to an end when my mother came to pick me up one day. She was early (which was noteworthy—with the exception of her job, my mom didn't generally "do" early). She was walking through the hallway of classrooms and came to a stop at my class. At that moment, I looked up from my desk to see her face pressed up against the glass window of the classroom door. What she saw was me, looking like a Brown Incredible Hulk against the backdrop of these joyful ten-year-olds. But not the Hulk when he's raging. The Hulk when he is starting to calm down, just before he's about to turn back into Bruce Banner, groaning with discomfort and shaking his head from side to side. There I was, a sad, confused loser, void of any of my usual confidence. I'll never forget her looking through that window at me, witnessing the reality of the situation. We locked eyes, and I made an expression to say, *I TOLD YOU*. That moment, something I could have never acted out for her, marked the end of Sunday school. She pulled me out.

In my ten years of Sunday school, there are essentially three memories I have of the place.

The first is of the hockey we would play during our lunchtime. It was hockey played using our feet as sticks. Now, some might say, "Isn't that soccer?" Sure, you could say that. But our strong Canadian patriotism was already established, so we called it "foot hockey." The puck/ball we used was a pair of socks. Which means every Sunday, some kid—some gracious volunteer—would take off his socks and roll them into a tight ball that we'd kick around for an hour. As a parent, it pains me to think of a child who might be (a) running around barefoot in his shoes or boots for an hour, and (b) worse still, a kid later unrolling socks that have been kicked around by twenty kids on a playground for an hour, and putting them *back* on his feet. (Also, I'm a hundred percent certain that my own sons would be exactly the type to volunteer for such a thing.) I also think of the people who would have driven by the school and seen dozens of kids kicking around balled-up socks. "Look at those poor children! Henry, that school really doesn't have much of a sports budget!" Our sports cost as much as our imaginations: zero dollars.

Second, as a childhood chubbo, I'll always remember what we used to eat at Sunday school: Bugles and Orange Crush. That's right, the notoriously nutritionally dense Bugle chips and the thirst-quenching nectar of the gods, Orange Crush. And the school was buying Costco portions of both, long before Costco even existed! I'm not sure what was Islamic about either of these things, but we ate them so often and so much that I started to wonder if we were maybe paying homage to some village message schlepper of days gone by who delivered the word of God via bugle, but perhaps was beaten to within an inch of his life for interrupting one too many debaucherous shindigs. As he lay bleeding, passersby described his blood as neon orange, but also fizzy.

And finally, I remember this line that was repeated to us often: "You must respect God, your parents, and your teachers." In that order. It was hammered into us. *God, your parents, your teachers.* And you can bet those Sunday school teachers tried to shoehorn themselves into that last group, too. One particular man, Misbah, would never miss a chance to say, "Respect *all* your teachers. *We* are also your teachers." Dude, you're a literal carpet salesman who volunteers here for three and a half hours on a Sunday and belittles children for being left-handed. "Teacher" is a bit of a stretch.

And, though I may not have picked up any Arabic or learned my prayers properly, I do remember this beautiful message from my days in Sunday school: *God is kind. God is merciful. God is forgiving.* This was repeated with such regularity that I can't help but remember it. Truthfully, I think it gave me a feeling of security and comfort in the world. If there was a God, I liked his vibe. Also, I think it was clear by an early age that I was going to be a bit of a screw-up, so that "forgiving" aspect was immediately appealing.

My challenges with the Arabic language were only partly over when my mother pulled me out of Sunday school. For some reason it was still imperative that I finish the Quran, in Arabic. Two steps forward, one step back, it appeared. My pleas of "You're aware that I still don't understand any Arabic, right?" fell on deaf ears. And when I asked if there was a reason why she wanted me so desperately *not* to understand the Quran, she replied, "You should also read it later, in English." Sigh. And so, for the immediate time being, a search began for a private tutor with whom I could complete the holy book that I was taking far too long to finish.

Mom had to ask around the neighbourhood, quizzing the mothers of other degenerate young boys, where they were finishing the Quran. Through her careful surveying, she got the name of an older Pakistani gentleman named Lateef. When they met she called him "Maulvi Sahib," which, like "imam," suggests that someone is a respected religious leader. He immediately corrected her, saying he wasn't an Islamic scholar, and that she could just refer to him as Lateef Sahib—*Sahib*, meaning "sir" or "mister." Not a scholar, and proudly opening with that info? *My man! I already have more in common with you than anyone else who's ever taught me the Quran.* For all of us young kids, he immediately became Lateef Uncle.

At first, it was a shared tutoring session. In his small apartment, I sat in the kitchen with some other kid across the table, and sometimes there might be a third child reading at a desk in a bedroom, the simultaneous drone of poorly enunciated Arabic coming from all of us. But once Lateef Uncle saw that I was going to require more guidance than the average kid (I *was* a tall fifteen-year-old boy at this point, so I couldn't fault him for assuming I'd be more competent than I was), my tutoring became private. He helped me finish the Quran—I wasn't afforded any other option—but that's not what stands out most in my memory. I remember two things about Lateef Uncle.

One was his insane cough. He was a small, frail man, maybe 130 pounds "soaking wet," as they say, and he was suffering from *something*. He may have actually told me, but to a fifteen-year-old idiot, emphysema, pertussis, and tuberculosis all blend into the same word. The important point is that his cough sounded like a combination of whooping, hacking, and wheezing all at the same time. And when he coughed, his frail body shook and shook so much that I often wished the Quran in front of me had been a CPR manual instead, because I was panicked that every day would be his last. To this day, whenever I hear that saying "He died doing what he loved," I realize that this was exactly what I was thinking at that kitchen table: if he goes, right here beside me, his family will have some comfort knowing that he went doing what he loved, helping a child read the Quran. The child in question, however, was going to be scarred with layers of trauma for the rest of his life.

To help with whatever condition plagued with him, Uncle had been prescribed an inhaler (it wasn't *just* asthma, I can guarantee that), and for anyone else, that should have been good news. With regards to Lateef Uncle, however, it was a completely irrelevant piece of equipment, because every time he put that inhaler to his mouth, he would press down on the top, and then *exhale*, spraying what might have been asthma medication everywhere, especially onto my arms and the back of my neck as I sat to his side, struggling to read the holy book. That said, maybe I'm being ungrateful. Maybe all those months of him spraying that medication into my pores is the reason I don't have asthma today!

Over the months that I was there—particularly as I went from shared tutoring to private tutoring—Lateef Uncle and I got to talking a little more freely. It was mostly me stalling to read in my pitiful Arabic, but I also found him to be a very kind man and I was genuinely interested in his own children and family. He would talk about his adult son, his grandkids, and even his wife, who had passed away. That would leave a chasm of silence in the kitchen and then finally he would say, "Okay! That's enough—your mother isn't paying me to talk about myself. Back to the Quran."

One day, my fears for his life had gotten the best of me and I decided I would have to let him know about this inhaler "situation."

"Uncle."
"Yes?"
"Umm . . . I think you might be using your *in*haler incorrectly
    [extra emphasis on the *in*]."
"Is that *right?*"
"I think when you press down on the button you might be
    breathing out, instead of breathing in."
"Is *that* right?"

Uncle, that's one hundred percent right. I felt like saying, "Exhibit A: the back of my neck." He considered my suggestion, and I watched him wrap his lips around the inhaler, press down on the button, and suck in the medication. I'll never forget that moment: his eyes just lit up! It was the first time he had ever tasted his own medicine! It was like watching a small child taste soda for the first time. After that day, I was his pal. My mother would drop me off at his little apartment and he would approach us at the door with a spring in his step, proclaiming in his slight Indo-Pakistani accent, "There's the guy. THERE'S the guy!" and then squeeze my shoulders. My mother even asked me what this sudden friendship was all about. "No big deal, Mom. Pretty much saved the guy's life. I'm a hero, that's all. Hey, maybe a hero could skip a Quran lesson from time to time?" But of course, no. No one missed a Quran lesson under my mother's watch.

The other thing I remember about Lateef Uncle was his unbelievable patience. He would rock back and forth with his eyes closed and mouth the words that we were supposed to be saying. He'd often have to correct a student's word or the pronunciation of it so that it didn't mean something completely different.

Over the years, God only knows what kind of similar mistakes I've made in Arabic. God and Lateef Uncle. But Uncle's role was to manage those mistakes. Unfortunately for him, I made a mistake every four or five words. He really earned his money when he was tutoring me.

When I finally completed the Quran, thanks almost entirely to this private tutoring, you'd think that seventeen-year-old me might have wanted to throw a party or go out for a meal with my family to celebrate, but it was more of a *Thank God that's over and done with* vibe in the house.

Yet, oddly, there are times to this day when I feel like I cheated my children out of something by not sending them to Sunday school. However much of a struggle it was for me, I still formed lifelong friendships and made strong memories. It seems like I only blocked the learnings I did on Sunday, not the socializing. But, for better or worse, because of my mom's strictness, or perhaps despite it, I broke with the long-standing tradition of ensuring that my kids learn how to read something in a language and not understand any of it.

Eventually I did read the Quran in English, and I hope my children do, as well. I mean, imagine someone saying they are a rock and roll guitarist, but never playing "Stairway to Heaven." Or someone who claims to be a French chef but doesn't know how to make a basic béchamel or hollandaise sauce. It's unthinkable. And so, if my kids are going to call themselves Muslims, they should really read the formative, foundational piece of Islamic work. The good news is, the Quran is something we own; it is in our house. Yes, it's in the high cupboard above the fridge. I just checked. And when they are ready and curious, they know where to find it.

Chapter 5

THE COMMUNITY

IN THE LATE 1980s, my family was living in Montreal, Quebec. And I mean, we were *living*. If you know your Canadian history, you'll be aware that in that time, Quebec was basically a lawless province. Stop signs and speed limits were mere suggestions heeded only by tourists and the very elderly; you could eat hot dogs and poutine for breakfast at numerous restaurants and diners across the province; and at the behest of singer Corey Hart, many locals had taken to wearing sunglasses at night. And the Hassan family of Brossard, Quebec, were enjoying all that this province had to offer to its fullest (Islamic Sunday school notwithstanding). Until, that is, my father dropped a bombshell on us one evening over dinner. He told us he had accepted a two-year contract to teach English—in Saudi Arabia.

If you knew my father, that's even odder than it sounds. Above and beyond his teaching profession, he was very much a freethinker: a poet, a short story writer, a creative person, a socialist, a supporter of all the freedoms, and, most important, the man liked his booze. Which is why we were all the more baffled about his interest in moving to Saudi Arabia, the mecca for, well—the place where Mecca is—AND where drinking alcohol is a punishable crime! How could he want this for himself? How could the social animal who loved arts and entertainment, the man who flocked to multiple screenings at the Montreal Film Festival every year with or without friends, who sat with the newspaper, circling all the Montreal Jazz Fest events he would attend—how could that man be interested in moving to Saudi Arabia?

There was only one explanation, and I had to ask directly: "Dad, how much do you hate Quebec?" He replied, "No, no, I just need a break from the cold." And a few seconds later, "And these bloody Frenchies!" He added "Frenchies," I can't lie about that. I don't know what they did to him, but it must have been unpleasant. My father embraced every single thing that Montreal had to offer—the aggressive drinking, the music, the smoked meat and bagels, the culture—just not the language. And given that he was a linguist, it was strange as all hell to observe.

This man understood the grammar and sentence structure of *multiple* languages. When I needed help with my French homework and was trying to determine the past participle or conditional subjunctive of any French verb, I could depend on him to look at it, write down the answer on a piece of paper, and slide it over to me. Slide it over—he wouldn't speak a word of it. He didn't want to give *them* the satisfaction. But wouldn't *you* get some satisfaction from being understood in the province you live in, Dad? Apparently not. And so, with an unyielding grudge toward Quebec's French and a contempt for its weather, he moved himself to Saudi Arabia.

There was talk (a short one) of us *all* perhaps moving. I would go to a boarding school in Europe, since there was no education higher than grade ten for non-locals in Saudi Arabia, and my mother and sister would live in the city of Medina with my father. I believe I had what was referred to at the time as a "hissy fit," and my mother uttered some kind of "Over my dead body will I leave my city, my work, and my friends to be part of this harebrained idea of yours" sentiment to my father. And so, he departed on his solo mission, and we were largely without his company for what turned out to be two and a half years.

We first went to visit Saudi Arabia after my father had already been there for six months. Prior to that, I'd only get to hear my father's voice if I was lucky enough to be in the house on the one or two occasions that he made a very expensive call home to Montreal. But, largely, my relationship with my dad consisted of letter writing. Letters felt so formal compared to the way we spoke to one another, and I think part of me was concerned that he'd send my letter back with red ink running across my grammatical mistakes and a mark out of ten. But his main interest, in true professorial form, was to have his son write more and read more.

It's wild to think of a time before cell phones and email, but also no internet meant we had a limited knowledge of Saudi Arabia. I could only know as much as I could find in the *Encyclopedia Britannica* on our shelves, and that edition was already eight years old. But aside from dated facts about global oil production and arid soil, we knew what most Muslims knew: it was the birthplace of Islam and the country to where every Muslim is required to make a pilgrimage (known as hajj) at least once in their lives. We also knew that it was hot, but when we touched down in Riyadh and the plane door opened out to the tarmac, it was quite literally the same gust of heat I'd get opening the oven door while baking french fries. And this was in December.

Saudi Arabia—have you been? Oh, you *must* go! It's lovely, especially this time of year, with the changing colours of the . . . sand. All right, early spoiler alert: I did not care for Saudi Arabia. And "did not care for" means I thought it was an awful place. And not the land or the geography of the place—no, I'm talking exclusively about the people running it. As a teen, I got to visit my father there three times, so I'm talking from a place of some experience. (The one time my mother and sister left me behind in Montreal, I threw a house party. Plants were puked in. Firecrackers were lit indoors. Police were called. You know, a party.) As a teen who was already struggling with his identity and his place in the world as a Muslim, I think it's fair to say that Saudi Arabia was the worst place to which I could have gone. Too many Saudi men behaved like women were beneath them. Many of us know how long it took women to get the right to drive in Saudi Arabia (*very* recently), and how women aren't allowed to walk with men who aren't their husbands, but beyond that, most men wouldn't even look my mother in the eye when she asked them a question. They would hear her, and then turn to me and say, "Tell your mother that the customs office is down this hallway . . ." Yeah, I don't think I'll need to do that, since she's a foot away from you and has perfect hearing.

And the treatment of non-Saudis was also confusing and irksome for me. If you read or watch the news, you're consistently led to believe that Muslims all around the world are a unified force. You hear about the "Muslim community" doing this, or about "the Muslim world" doing that. Statements like that are complete rubbish because (a) no community is a monolith. I mean, even in Canada we would never recognize Canadians as a monolith! Would anyone in this country accept someone saying, "Maritimers . . . Quebecers. Same shit." Or "You're from Saskatchewan, right? Oh, Alberta. Well . . . same difference." For the love of God, the people in Kelowna, B.C., and West Kelowna, B.C., separated by only a swimmable valley of water, don't even want to be compared to each other! So no, the roughly two billion Muslims in this world, spread across a hundred countries, speaking hundreds of different languages and coming from hundreds of different ethnic backgrounds, are most certainly not all the same. And (b) the Muslim "community," *were it* to act like one, could literally not build a sandcastle together. I can't emphasize this enough: there is no unity in this group. And there's nothing like a visit to Saudi Arabia to confirm that for you.

The best way to illustrate the dynamic of how things work for Muslims there is to think of a chicken coop. The Saudis are at the top, sitting pretty and shitting on everything below them. One level under the Saudis are the Gulf Arabs, just experiencing a wee bit of shit from above. Under them are all the other Arabs. Here, there are more significant droppings. But right at the bottom, experiencing a rainfall of shit, are all the other Muslims from countries like India, Pakistan, Bangladesh, the Philippines, Indonesia. (And where are the white people, some of you might be asking? Right on top, riding shotgun with the Saudis. That's a very healthy relationship, in case you were concerned.) This was all a few years before I started studying political science; I knew next to nothing at the time about globalism and the relationships that the Saudis had with Western energy companies, but what I did see was enough to know I didn't like it there.

My childhood friends who had lived in Saudi Arabia always spoke about the corporate compounds they lived in—a small, gated neighbourhood, effectively, with a grocery store, an exercise facility, games rooms, populated by well-to-do expats and their families. Unfortunately, as a teacher, my father had no such arrangement. He was on the main floor of a regular old building in a one-bedroom apartment, right in the thick of Medina. He had a few colleagues and one very hospitable student that might drop in, but none of them had children whom my sister and I could socialize with. Our days consisted of watching *Kojak* (one of the few shows that the Saudi censors allowed in), going to the local corner store, eating delicious shawarma, and going to the mosque every night for prayers.

Rumour had it that the Saudis had hired officials whose job it was to make sure all the employees of the university, regardless of which country they hailed from (they were all Muslim), were regularly attending prayers. One of my father's first friends, a teacher from Pakistan, had a personal visit from these officials. They knocked on his door and told him he should be attending mosque more often. He responded with an "I pray at home" (probably not true), and also, "And when I do, it's none of your damned business." They responded two weeks later by firing him and sending him back home. The message was clear: If you want to work here, you will do as we do. My dad had left Quebec, where the language police were a constant source of harassment, for a country that had a prayer police! THIS is what it took to get my father to the mosque.

Possibly the least exciting thing we learned about Saudi Arabia was that, in the 1980s, it was the only country—in a cruel irony—which required not only an entry visa but also an exit visa. So essentially, as soon as you landed you had to immediately start working toward the process of leaving, by arranging for that exit visa. Like, dude, I'm not sure I even want to be here to begin with, and now I gotta fill out paperwork to get out of here? I didn't have to fill out the paperwork, my father did, but I was offended on his behalf.

They may still do the exit visa thing in SA. I don't know, I don't need to know, and most important, I certainly didn't want to google that. I know how that goes. One search about "Saudi travel visas" and next thing you know, it's "Sexy Saudi singles want to meet you!" pop-up ads in my browser. Or much worse, "Click here for the latest stoning vids" from some Saudi WorldStarHipHop equivalent. Hard pass, thank you.

Each time we visited, my father and I would go to this government office to start the exit visa process. "Office" is maybe a strong word for what it was. A Booster Juice in a shopping plaza is five times the size of that government office. Inside, three men sat behind a long counter, doing an incredible amount of nothing. My father would speak first, always. If you think there was any semblance of a "Hi, how are you today, how can we help?" you are picturing the wrong place.

"Hi, we are here to inquire about our exit visas."

They would just stare at us (size us up) for an uncomfortably long time, and finally the Alpha Loser of the group would break the silence:

"*Come back Tweesday.*"
"Oh, sure. Yes, we could certainly do that. But you probably want
    to know our family name so you can look it up: it's Hassan."
"*Tweesday.*"
"Okay, so if we come back 'Tweesday,' it'll be ready?"
"*Inshallah.*"

You son of a mother—I know what that means! And it was rarely a good thing to hear in Saudi Arabia. Inshallah, if you're not aware, means "God willing." A beautiful term, at its heart. If you're a God-fearing person, it's a saying that conveys a message that you are not alone in this world, that God is shepherding over you as you go through your journey in life. Furthermore, it is a term that the Saudis absolutely *ruined* for me in those visits. "Your visa will be ready, *inshallah*"—this doesn't have anything to do with Allah! This could just involve you, getting off your fat ass and stamping something and it'll be ready. I know you're very busy using that letter opener to pick something out of the back of your teeth, sir, but certainly we don't have to involve God in this one. I'm sure he's got other stuff to deal with!

But hey, if I never go back to Saudi Arabia, I'll never have to hear it again, right? Incorrect. It happens, in fact, to be the most overused and often misused term in the Muslim world. Often, "inshallah" is just the equivalent of your mom's "We'll see" to your twelve-year-old self. And this asshole, in this government office/closet in late-1980s Saudi Arabia, was *definitely* pulling a mom's

"We'll see." I'm not asking for a bike for Christmas or permission to go to the grade seven semiformal dance, bud. I simply want to get out of this country.

I have an uncle in Cambridge, Ontario—he is the purveyor of many, many inshallahs. He'll bookend every sentence with the word and throw extras in the middle for good measure.

"*Inshallah*, I will go to the travel agent *inshallah* tomorrow at two
   p.m., *inshallah*."
"Okay, I'll see you there."
"Tsk-tsk, *inshallah!*"

What? You have to micromanage *my* inshallahs, too? You've dished out enough to go around for all of us! Even a twenty-second chat with him is a traumatic reminder of the Saudis. "Ali? *Inshallah*, I will call you right back, *inshallah*." Come on, man, how bad is your luck that you don't think you're going to make a call back to me in two minutes? How bad is your health? Are you downing shots of ghee every morning?

We should do one daily inshallah. ONE. First thing in the morning, we just look up and go, "*Inshallah*, all day, on everything." While Muslims are on our fiftieth inshallah of the day, Jews and Christians are doing all kinds of wonderful things with all the free time they have on their hands. We're wasting precious time over here! Saudi Arabia ruined *inshallah*, they treated us non-Saudis like third-class citizens, and they treated women like something even less than that.

Over the course of my life, I've watched a number of people go to Saudi Arabia and come back "changed." More than one family friend went there as a drinker, saw "the light," and never touched alcohol again. Saudi Arabia can have that effect. The pilgrimage to Mecca is an especially incredible scene. That pilgrimage, oddly, is one of the few pillars of Islam that I've been able to follow. I say oddly, because it's something that most Muslims save and plan for their entire lives, and I've done it *twice*, as a teenager! (Mind you, it's pretty easy when your dad has moved to Saudi Arabia and you're paying him semiannual visits.) But experiencing hajj, or *umrah* (the scaled-down version that I did, outside the month of Ramadan)—in which thousands or millions of people are all unified, subservient, and praying to the same God at the exact same time—can be a breathtakingly powerful experience. And it can leave you with only the most positive memories of Saudi Arabia. Or, you can have an entirely different type of experience.

If you're a fifteen-year-old and you lose your father to a different country, you want to be able to see that country and say to your father, "I get it. I get why you moved here. I get why you moved away from your teen son, your young daughter, and your wife for an extended period of time. I see why you *need* to be here." But I didn't. I didn't get it at all. I still don't. The most social, progressive man I knew left his friends and his ideals for *this*? Was this a midlife crisis? Why not just buy a convertible like the dads on television?

There was a greater language barrier in Saudi Arabia than there was in Quebec. There was a scorching heat that was far worse than any cold Canada could create. This was also a country that quite openly had no respect for him, save for a few kind students and colleagues. Ironically, my father's exodus to the birthplace of Islam made my (and his) connection to the religion shakier than it already was.

Chapter 6

I'M PRETTY FLEXIBLE IN THAT DEPARTMENT

My dearest Peppi,

I hope my letter finds you well. This past month has been awful without you. Please know that I do think about you often. My heart aches at the thought of us not being reunited soon. Mother says we don't belong together, but you mustn't pay her any mind. She comes from a different time and place, where affairs such as yours and mine were uncommon. You will always be . . . my Pepperoni.

THE CONSUMPTION OF PORK is forbidden in Islam. The interesting thing is that it's also forbidden in Judaism. Frankly, I think that this could be the most underappreciated and overlooked tool in the struggle for Muslim-Jewish unity. I mean, don't you see it guys? It's the old "The enemy of my enemy is my friend" thing! Stand together against your common foe! That said, it would appear that the animosity between Jews and the pig has been decreasing steadily over time. For a number of years, I hosted a Christmastime comedy show with a roster of Muslim and Jewish comedians, cleverly titled "Kosher Jokes for the Halaladays." I can't take any credit for that name—that was the genius of my friends Eman and Jess—but it was a rare and treasured moment to be in a room with many Muslims and Jews simultaneously, and I took the opportunity to launch into my own personal surveying:

"How many Jewish people are here right now?"

[*Cheers.*]

"Okay, and how many of you eat pork?"

[*Cheers.*]

"All right. And how many Muslims here right now?"

[*Cheers.*]

"Okay, and how many of *you* eat pork?"

[*Utter and complete silence.*]

"See, this is interesting. Who was Jewish here that eats pork?"

[*Hand goes up.*]

"Okay, tell me: Are Jews technically allowed to eat pork?"

"No."

"And yet you do. Why is that?"

[*Shoulder shrug.*] "Mehhh . . ."

This was a revelation to me. Because I rarely found a *Mehhh* in Islam. Certainly not when it comes to pork. One time, while in Atlanta, I went to visit a friend named Faiz at his apartment. As we were chatting, I let out that I ate pork and he thought it was hilarious. He also felt it was imperative that I tell his cousin—a nineteen-year-old visiting from India who was camped out on Faiz's couch, high out of his brains, playing *Tetris* on a big-screen television.

"Hey, Samir, Ali has something to tell you." *Do I, though? We could probably skip it. Okay, I guess*—"I eat pork." Samir just froze for a second, then paused the game and stood up (with great difficulty). He looked at me with parental-level disappointment in his eyes and said, "You eat pork, man? Bro. BRO. That's the *unforgivable sin.*"

Two things about that. First, no it's not. I actually looked it up and this kid was doing some major editorializing from the Good Book. And second, I've still never ruined someone's vibe quite like I did that day. I completely killed the buzz of a kid who'd been smoking weed for at least seven hours with the news of my pork consumption. I don't know where that guy is now or what he's become, but I can tell you that he will *never* be ready to hear the news that I was a judge at a Ribfest.

Point is, if there was ever a time for a fellow Muslim to shrug off my pork consumption with a friendly *Mehhh*, that was it. It just doesn't happen.

That's a rallying cry for another time, perhaps, but you should know that pigs are prohibited because they have a cloven hoof and don't chew their cud—partly digested food that returns from the stomach to the mouth for further chewing (as if that is somehow desirable). And thus, for hoof- and regurgitation-related reasons, the pig is deemed unfit for consumption and unclean. You think I understand that? I don't. Which is why you are finding what is effectively a love letter to pork this early in a book written by a Muslim. It's really too early. When I performed my live show at a comedy festival in Edinburgh, a Pakistani father-and-son duo left as soon as I started talking about pork. *"But why? It's so delicious!"* you're screaming into the abyss. Hardly the point, my friends.

I'm a relatively late adopter in this pork world. I was sixteen when *she* came into my life. And I like to call her "she," because "it" just isn't respectful enough. And she deserves respect! Many of you won't get that, because you've taken her for granted. Your mother probably crumbled bacon bits in your baby food when you were a child and now you talk about her like some old relic that you don't even appreciate! But not I. No, I give her the respect she deserves.

If we revisit the congenital limitations that I discussed earlier, shouldn't I as a Muslim, preceded by generations of Muslims, have a natural distaste for pork? You'd certainly think so, but apparently not. In fact, I loved pepperoni before I even tasted it. Allow me to explain how that happened.

In my high school, it always felt like if you stayed after school for an activity, you were rewarded with pizza. This activity could be something that involved actually being active, like track and field, or it could have involved almost no movement, like the Yearbook Club. But whoever you were and whatever extracurricular thing you did, if you stayed after school, you were almost always guaranteed nourishment via pizza. And what kind of pizza was it? Pepperoni. Every single time. It was like there was no other option. No one asked about your ethnic background or your religion or requested your allergy report.

I always wondered if there was a conversation like this happening in the faculty room:

Concerned Teacher 1: But, Mr. Ingall, what if the children are Muslim?

Mr. Ingall: They can remove the pepperoni.

Concerned Teacher 1: But, Mr. Ingall, what if the children are vegetarian?

Mr. Ingall: They can remove the pepperoni.

Concerned Teacher 1: But, Mr. Ingall, what if the children are vegan?

Mr. Ingall: They can remove— Wait. What the hell is a vegan, Dolores? It's 1989! A vegan? They can be homeschooled!

That's not meant to be a jab on veganism. I'm just saying, if you were a vegan in 1989—come on. Too soon! That was a cold, hard world for a vegan. That was a bubble boy situation. You stayed in your house and let people bring things to *you*. You didn't walk the street talking about your veganism, for God's sake—you'd be stuffed in a locker for a month! I know this may not make sense to young readers. We live now in a world where someone can say, "I am on an ovo-lacto, pescatarian, ketogenic, gluten-free, low FODMAP diet, so please respect me and my journey," and not only do people not fall over laughing, but they help them out. The eighties and nineties were unforgiving when it came to diet.

I wound up staying after school a fair bit. Volleyball. Debating. Detention. I had a wide variety of interests. But any time I *did* get that slice of pizza, I removed that pepperoni, because I was a Muslim, and that's what we did. But every time I did, you could inevitably catch me staring at my slice of now-cheese pizza, thinking: *Wow. There are remnants of something very special here in these circular indentations. One day. One day I will investigate your origins.*

But most important, I removed the pepperoni because my close buddy, Faisal Shahabuddin, was Muslim, too. Though, to simply say he was Muslim doesn't do the situation justice. He was a Muslim wunderkind. Muslim parents would stare at their children with great disappointment and yell, "Why can't you be more like Faisal?"

I'll give you one example of this kid. In my teens, Ramadan landed in the summer. Islam follows the lunar calendar, so an Islamic calendar year, while still having twelve months, is shorter than the Gregorian calendar year by about ten days. In my life, the month of Ramadan has fallen in every single "white calendar" month. If you know a little something about Islam, you likely know that Ramadan is a month of fasting. We are supposed to eat and drink absolutely nothing from sunup to sundown for thirty days (well, approximately thirty—the moon can be moody). I've seen Ramadan in February, where you abstain from eating from about 7 a.m. to 3:45 p.m. in Eastern Canada. Which is exactly when I started thinking, *Maybe I should start fasting again—I could do this!* I still didn't, for some reason.

As it happened, in my teens, Ramadan overlapped with the month of July. No cushy, fat-cat dead-of-winter fasting period—no. These were long, hot days. The month of July in Montreal, steamy and sweltering, makes 31 degrees Celsius feel more like 40. And fifteen-year-old Faisal Shahabuddin would fast, for fifteen and a half hours, while playing hours of basketball with us in the unforgiving heat. Not a drop of water, and not a morsel of food. And that's why we couldn't be more like Faisal—because he was a robot. By his early teens, he already had the discipline of a trained monk. So, no, I couldn't eat pepperoni in front of that guy. But one day, I knew I would have to try it.

Like so many teens, I didn't like being told what to do. It's remained a struggle to this day, to the point that I don't even like telling other people what to do! That's what has made me such a bad manager in the past (please let me believe that this is the reason). But loving food and then being told there was something I wasn't "allowed" to eat particularly didn't jibe well. It bothered me to my very core to have someone on my back saying, "What is that? Is that pork? Look at the ingredients. Does it have pork in it? You aren't allowed to eat pork!" All right, take it easy! What are you, *my mom*? It was my mom. Still, I didn't like it. And come on, Mom, your first true friends when you moved to this country were Crisco and butter. You force-fed me every single thing Betty Crocker encouraged you to make, turned me into the chubby child I was, and now you're telling me there is something seemingly incredible out there that I *can't* eat?

And so, my one day came. I was without my friend Faisal. I think I was on some high school dance committee, and Faisal was not allowed at after-school dance committee meetings, never mind dances. It was my chance. It was the moment I had privately fantasized about over and over again.

You might be wondering, *Weren't you sixteen? Why didn't you just do whatever the hell you wanted to do? Grab a slice, look around at whomever, and just announce, "Guys, I'm not religious anymore, I'm spiritual now!" and take a damned bite?*

Oh ho-ho! Would that I could have done such a thing! What a simple world that would have been. But that's not at all what we are dealing with here. Muslims, you see, have a very complicated relationship with pork. It is *the* line for the vast majority of Muslims. I have met Muslims who have developed an incredible personal level of comfort with consuming alcohol (not allowed), doing drugs (get your shit together), stealing (how dare you), and who never fast during Ramadan (oh, the horror)—but they will never, *ever* eat pork.

I have a cousin—true story—who tried crack one summer. This bored suburban teen tried crack. More than once, too. But you can't pay that guy to have a BLT. There's just not enough money in the world. I was with him once at a diner when the wrong order was plopped down in front of him—it was clearly some kind of bacon-laden sandwich. His eyes widened and his voice actually started to quiver: "I didn't order that. I didn't order that!" Okay, take it easy man. *This* makes you nervous? You remember the summer of *crack*? Let's get some perspective here. We'll send the bad sandwich back. Stop hyperventilating.

My cousin is hardly alone in this. One of my Muslim friends, Shammy, is an extremely focussed, committed, and hardworking consultant—for five days a week. On the weekends, he takes that same focus, commitment, and work ethic with him to nightclubs and house parties. Years later, I can still say I haven't met anyone with Shammy's stamina. When I lived in Chicago, he'd be wasted every weekend, and at 3 a.m., we'd inevitably find ourselves heading to a Chinese restaurant—partly because they were the only ones still open, but mainly in the hopes that some heavy, greasy food would sober him up. As soon as our server would approach us, some kind of Muslim lightbulb would go off in Shammy's head. The fact that he was almost blind with alcohol poisoning was still no match for his years of indoctrination. He would yell at the waiter,

"No pork on my fork, okay? NO PORK ON MY FORK!" Really, man? No pork on your fork? Do you remember last night? Your Muslim ass certainly wasn't yelling, "NO WHORE AT MY DOOR!" when it should have.

Also in Chicago, I had made friends with an Indian Muslim colleague whose desk was directly across from the company's boardroom. Every time a meeting let out she would walk over to my desk and whisper the words "Their meeting's over" into my cubicle—God bless her. Those words were my cue to join her on a nonchalant saunter (read: the most exciting part of my day) to the boardroom for a plethora of leftover pizza that none of the execs cared to touch. Each time, she would say to me, "Be careful, some of these might have pork on them." At first, I'd sneakily take a pepperoni slice and quickly cover it with a vegetarian one before she could notice, but eventually I just decided to tell her that I was comfortable eating pork. My line was "I'm pretty flexible in the pork department." You might say that what I lacked in hip and knee flexibility I was trying to make up for with my mouth and stomach. Her response to me was "Oh, I'm not. *I'm a good girl.*" And I'm not saying she wasn't a "good girl," but I *am* saying that more than once I found myself helping to hold her hair back while she vomited outside a nightclub. And no, it wasn't food poisoning.

I share this to help illustrate one of the more controversial opinions I've held in the Muslim community (and I've had a number of them): I can't help but think that somewhere along the way we got too hung up on the poor pig. I mean, are families being torn apart by pork addictions? *"Johnny spends all his money on ham and there's nothing left for the children!" "You let Brenda drive after eating all that pulled pork? You know how she gets after she's eaten a few!"* I don't think so.

But whatever my opinion about the subject, the fact remained that being a Muslim teenager who simply chooses to eat pork in front of other Muslims was a near impossibility. As a Muslim, you have your own guilt to contend with. Then there's your friend's potential horror. If he tells his parents—because he needs someone to talk to about it—*they'll* judge you. Harshly. If it gets out to the community, *they'll also* be disgusted by you. And then when it gets back to your parents, you'll have to face *their* disappointment. It's too much! You have to eat it in the dark, beside a dumpster, ready to throw it out at a moment's notice. "What? Me? Oh, I was just eating some tobacco I found on the ground." You'd literally be better off saying *that* than admitting it was pork.

And yet, on that day, at that high school dance committee meeting, and after much deliberation, I did not remove the pepperoni. I remember it glistening. It was always glistening. I remember bringing the slice to my face and looking at it. Time kind of stopped. I vaguely recall my buddy Lee in the background asking me, "Hey, Ali, can I have your pepperoni?" *Not today, you bastard.* And then I bit into that slice of pepperoni pizza. I still shudder as I think about it. WOW. (A) Delicious. (B) Thrilling! It was quite literally *the* forbidden fruit! (Putting aside the fact that it is quite literally not fruit.) But really, when was the last time you ate something that fit *that* description: delicious *and* thrilling? The best way I can describe it is this: when you eat pork as a Muslim teen for the first time, you feel like you're on the run from the law.

At that very moment, I was hooked. From that day forward, whenever the opportunity was presented to me—and there were no prying Muslim eyes around—I ate pork. Now, to be clear, I was filled with guilt. But I was also filled with pork.

But there *was* guilt. Something evidently did get in my brain when I was in those Islamic school classes. I couldn't quite extricate from my mind the fact that pork was *haram* (forbidden).

If I'm being completely transparent, the vast majority of Muslims I met really didn't care that I ate pork. I'd deliver my well-rehearsed "I'm flexible on the pork issue" line, and they'd say, "That's cool, man. Enjoy hell. Anyway, wanna play some hacky sack?" and we'd move on with our day together. But if you've ever given a speech to a hundred people and three weren't listening, you tend to fixate on those three, and not the ninety-seven heroes in the room. That's what happened to me. I met just a handful of people who hinted at, suggested, or outright said that I was a bad Muslim or person, and made me feel like I had committed some kind of irreparable damage to my community and society at large. At some point in my early twenties, my insecurity gave rise to my immaturity, and my feeling became "Fine, I don't want to be part of your dumb club anyway!"

By the time I was in my late twenties, I had fully crossed over to the "other side." I would stroll through grocery aisles, pulling certain meats out of the fridge with interest—"Ooh, ribs! Oh, *beef* ribs? Never mind"—and then putting them back. As comedian Ramy Youssef has said, "Every Muslim has their own line, their own code." My religious code was loosening to the point where I might have even started becoming a bad Christian.

I am precisely zero percent impressed with kids who grow up in Pakistan or Dubai and say, "Well, I don't eat pork." Yeah, no shit—you know how many hoops you have to jump through just to find it in your respective countries? Big deal! Try going on a school trip to a *cabane à sucre* in 1980s Quebec and tell me how easy it is to avoid pork. Eggs? Fried in bacon fat. Bread? Made with lard. Pea soup? Made with ham hocks. Sausages? Pork in a pork casing. The famous Québécois meat pie, *tourtière*? It's pork that makes it famous. *Here, kid, enjoy a few tablespoons of maple syrup while every one of your classmates bathes in pork fat.*

I watched this happen right before my own eyes in the mid-nineties when I went on my fourth or fifth trip to this same type of sugar shack, this time with the Indo-Canadian Students Association of McGill. Before we left, I pulled my friend Arsalaan aside and told him, "By the way, I grew up in this province, bro. The food at these places is pretty, how you say, pork-heavy." Poor, sweet, naive Arsalaan responded with "Oh, I'm sure I'll find something to eat." There really wasn't anything that could have prepared him—and another Muslim student named Nila—for what they walked into that afternoon.

At these sugar shack day trips, they have you do a number of hours of walking and hiking in the snow before lunch, so you build up quite an appetite. The smell of that lunch hall alone would have toppled over most Muslims. Even I, occasional pork eater that I was by that time, found it all pretty intense: picture a sauna, and on those hot sauna rocks, bacon is sizzling and creating a salty, porky haze in the air. That was the cafeteria. We all watched, wide-eyed, as multiple platters of food arrived, making us feel like kings and queens at a regal banquet (we hadn't gotten out much yet).

Arsalaan tried not to be a bother, but Nila walked over to the large square window leading into the kitchen and said to a big, burly French Québécois man with tattoos on his arms—long before such a look was trendy—as politely and sweetly as she possibly could, "Excuse me, sir, is there pork in anything?" I'll never forget him slamming his knife down and shouting, "Dere's pork in hevery-ting, madame!"

Once, in an act of Muslim teen rebellion and defiance, I ordered a pepperoni pizza to our house. (I was probably eighteen years old, so yeah, a little too old for rebellion, but no one ever accused me of being quick to mature.) I was going to watch *Saturday Night Live* and eat a pepperoni pizza and, dammit, no one could tell me I couldn't! My sister saw the pizza and was immediately grossed out by me. The force was strong in this one, a *Star Wars* nerd might say. Also, the snitch was strong in this one, and she ratted me out to the higher-ups. My mother was furious, but struggled to respond to my defence: "Why not? We drink in this house. That's not allowed in Islam. So why not eat pepperoni?" She eventually came up with "I don't want pork in this house, it stinks!" which felt like a small victory. Then my father approached me calmly and used a different tack: "Look, Ali, it's true—pork and alcohol are both not supposed to be consumed in Islam. And so why do we allow one in this house and not the other, I get it. But rather than focus on that, think about this—I have heart disease, on your mother's side there's a lot of heart disease. Pork is just not a great choice from a fat and cholesterol perspective. If you don't eat it regularly, maybe it's better not to start, for the sake of your health."

I sat there for a bit, digesting that argument and thinking about how awful it was to see my father hospitalized a year prior, courtesy of angina. *Also*, it was pretty surreal to get health advice from a man who had tried every form of tobacco for over thirty years—cigarettes, pipes, snuff, he even tried chewing tobacco when he "quit."

But look—I'm a glutton. In the end, I still ate some of that pizza, but I didn't finish it. And the part that I *did* eat didn't taste as good as it should have. Dad and his well-reasoned guilt trip ruined a perfectly good pizza that night.

As I raise my children in our quasi-Muslim home, I consider how I might react to them eating pork one day. I know my wife wouldn't be comfortable with that, but I have to say with all honesty it wouldn't bother me in the least. Like, actually zero. When and if they tell me they drink, on the other hand, there will certainly be cause for concern. I'll immediately wonder *how* will they drink. Will it be to excess? Will they be bad drunks? Will they be violent? Will they be irresponsible? Will they drive drunk? Will they get into alcohol-fuelled interactions with strangers? On the other hand, what's the worst thing that could happen from too much pork? You get the extra-meat-lovers' pizza and your heart stops beating for a few seconds? It'll start back up! I'd truly be far more content to introduce my kids to a little prosciutto than any alcohol at all, but unfortunately, that's the kind of talk that can get you excommunicated from your relatives and in-laws.

Chapter 7

THE FORBIDDEN FRUIT, LITE

BEER IS COLLOQUIALLY CALLED *MOOTTAR* in Punjabi. Which literally means "horse piss." I'm not sure how often horse piss comes up in conversation that we would need one special word for it, but I remember the first time I had a sip of beer. I must have been thirteen or fourteen. I had already had a few California Coolers in my time—it wasn't my first rodeo! But beer had always smelled prohibitively awful. The men were all in the basement drinking and chatting when my dad's buddy, Uncle Ilyas, suggested that I was old enough to give beer a try. His suggestion was inviting enough for me to agree, and I took a sip of something called John Labatt Classic.

That sip goes down in my history as the most repulsive thing I have ever tasted. "How could ANYONE ever want to drink this?" I asked aloud, in one of my more naive moments. What was wrong with my dad and uncles? What had died inside them all that this hideous beverage would provide them with comfort of any kind? In that moment, John Labatt made it painfully clear to me where and why the word *moottar* was needed. And worst of all, this was John's special stuff—it was the classic! Not that pedestrian Labatt Blue drivel that even he couldn't bring himself to attach his own image to.

As an aside, *"Moottar matt peena!"* (Don't drink horse piss!) became the words of my aunt as my cousin and I would "step out for a bit." Not what you'd call a *traditional* nugget of parental advice as you leave the house. Certainly not Muslim parental advice.

So, while I was raised in a Pakistani Muslim home, our values weren't super entrenched in the Muslim side of things. You've probably picked up on that by now. We went for Eid prayers twice a year, I went to Islamic Sunday school (with great reluctance), and we had lots of open-minded or similar-minded Muslim friends—but there certainly was drinking, mainly by my father. How much? Let me put it this way. When I was in my late teens, my mom had to loudly and aggressively lay down a rule: "No more alcohol in this house!" That should be an indication of where our family landed on the Muslim scale.

Sadly, that rule turned out to be a little bit myopic. Turns out she should have added, "No alcohol in the car, either!" We always thought that my dad was at the corner store having drinks in the back with the odd cast of characters who hung out there. Which he was. Or that he was at the bar. Which he was. We actually had a place called Cheers a few minutes' drive from our home. Same logo as the bar from the television show, similar layout—they must have been paying a fortune in franchise fees. But men like my father were clearly helping finance that. I knew he was at Cheers a fair amount because a few of my friends would tell me that they drove him home on various nights. One buddy driving my father's car, another buddy following behind in another car with my dad. That's an actual service now where I live. It's anywhere from fifty to a hundred dollars. And that lucky bugger was getting it for free, from guys I went to high school with.

But it turns out that my father had another place he drank, too: in the driver's seat of his 1989 Toyota Corolla. I only witnessed it once, and I'd love to believe that was the only time it happened. *I'd love to.* It was around eight o'clock on a beautiful summer evening, and my friend Sihai and I were Rollerblading in the neighbourhood. Photographers refer to that time as "the golden hour," as the sun is softer and redder in that period before it sets. Personally, I would have to describe that particular evening as less than golden. Sihai and I were about fifty yards from an intersection in our suburb, and perpendicular to us was a car approaching the stop sign. Sihai smiled and said, "Hey, isn't that your dad?" And at that very moment, as he came to a rolling stop (the classic "Québécois stop"), my father raised a can in a paper bag to his mouth, took a swig, and continued driving straight. He never looked our way; never even knew we were there.

I had so many issues with that interaction.

1. Sihai was my closest friend at the time, and he had no idea what kind of drinking my father did. It's pretty hard to deny that there's a problem when you see someone's dad drinking in his car *while* driving. "Oh that? He just gets thirsty sometimes. It was probably just a can of coconut water that he didn't want to take out of the brown paper bag. He doesn't want anyone to know about his electrolyte deficiency, so let's keep that just between us, okay?" That wasn't going to fly.

2. Jesus Christ, Dad, look both ways at a stop sign! That's what you're supposed to do as a driver. Another car or, God forbid, a cop, could have been at the other corner of the intersection where we were Rollerblading.

3. How badly did you need to drink? You couldn't have hidden in the basement or backyard? Found a park? Met your buddies at the corner store?

4. Technically, the sun *was* still up.

Because of all this, we've struggled in my home now to figure out how we should "present" alcohol to our children. If they start drinking while they are driving, realistically I'll be too old to chase them in my Rollerblades.

One option for us is complete transparency. I have tried this. I have, for example, removed a bottle of rum from the highest cupboard in the kitchen and poured a small glass for myself in front of the family. Honesty is the best policy, right? Not quite. My youngest son, pretty much as soon as he turned four, immediately started asking, "Can I have some?" No. "But can I just try it!" No. "But why can't I try it?" Because Mama and Papa will go to jail if anyone finds out we gave alcohol to a kid. "But how will they find out?" Good Lord, I don't know, but I don't trust any of you snitches and you can't drink this, end of story!

The other option has been to drink more covertly. One time, I had stationed a gin and tonic in a small mason jar at the back of the kitchen counter, and I was going back to it periodically to have a sip. No one was the wiser. As "luck" would have it, my daughter accidentally bit into a chili pepper in her supper and ran to the sink in a panic. Her mouth was burning so much that she literally couldn't even wait to pour or run the water, so she grabbed the first thing she could see on the counter. Can you imagine what gin tastes like to an eleven-year-old, especially when she's expecting water? She took a big gulp, spit it out immediately, and started screaming, "What is that? WHAT IS THAT!" She ran to the bathroom to wash out her mouth and came back in even more of a panic, yelling, "Am I an alcoholic now?"

The third option is of course to not drink at all, but I'm not ready for something quite so radical. I always hoped we'd be like a good old-fashioned Italian family—giving a little wine to my preteen children with dinner, so that by time they are teenagers they see no particular appeal in alcohol. I also remember the words of Mr. Moos when we were adolescents. He always said, "I don't mind the boys drinking, as long as they are doing it under my roof. It's what happens outside that I don't trust." Seems wise. But when I look into my youngest's gluttonous eyeballs, I don't trust that, either. I can't shake the feeling that he's going to be the kid pouring himself large glasses of wine with every meal by the time he's eight. For now, I'm reverting back to drinking on the down-low (and hiding the cup somewhere out of reach).

When it came to booze or pork, I was never able to understand the inconsistency or the double standard. I just couldn't wrap my head around this cop-out. If you're going to fully practise Islam, then do it. But you're going to judge me for eating pork when you do all this other stuff? Cutting pork is the easy one! Well, maybe not *so* easy in Quebec in the eighties, but still—why judge others if you're cheating with, say, alcohol? Clearly, I wasn't the only one who had some stuff to figure out.

Religion is supposed to be a compass—a constant in life that helps you make sense of everything else. But what happens when religion is what confuses you the most? In my youth, I essentially turned my back on the whole thing, but I can see now it left a hole—one I spent years filling with pretty much everything else I could be a part of.

Part 3
BELONGING

Chapter 8

HOME AND NATIVE LAND

THE FIRST TIME I WENT to Mexico was with my wife and kids, and it was an absolute thrill. Sure, it was "only" a three-star resort with moderately amusing nightly entertainment, but I didn't care. I was especially happy for my daughters and my son. "THIS is living," I said to myself between bites of bacon-wrapped plantain, merengue tutorials, and sips of rum and Coke with a quickly deteriorating paper straw. "We finally belong." And minus that straw, I really did love everything about that trip because it represented something I was never able to do when I was young.

The experience of most South Asians—at least when I was a young one— was that we didn't travel. I mean, we packed our bags, went to the airport, boarded a plane and flew in it—but we didn't "travel" in the classic sense. It certainly wasn't a vacation. It was an obligatory annual or semiannual return to the motherland.

It always confused me—so many of my friends were heading annually to Florida to rub elbows with Mickey Mouse, while my dad's singular focus was a trip to Pakistan. Even at a young age, I remember thinking, sure, relatives are great, but between the flights, the gifts that had to be purchased, and the money that was handed out when we were there, our family could have gone on a two-week trip to Thailand! Or New Zealand. Or Disneyland! Any other *land*! Some place, essentially, where I didn't have to squat to poo in a hole in the ground.

I remember one of the very few trips our family went on that didn't involve a visit to relatives: it was a drive from Montreal to upstate New York. On the first day, we visited the "famous" Lake George—the site of the Battle of Lake George of 1755. Apparently in 1791, Thomas Jefferson wrote in a letter to his daughter, that *"Lake George is without comparison, the most beautiful water I ever saw; formed by a contour of mountains into a basin . . . finely interspersed with islands, its water limpid as crystal, and the mountain sides covered with rich groves . . . down to the water-edge: here and there precipices of rock to checker the scene and save it from monotony,"* proving that Thomas Jefferson either smoked opium or ate mushrooms. It's just a lake and a rocky beach, dude. We stayed in a 2.5-star-ish motel overnight and then went to a place called "Ausable Chasm" the next morning. Look, I'm sure as far as chasms go, it's a lovely one. But at the end of the day, for fourteen-year-old Ali Hassan and his kid sister, no fissure or abyss or gorge (God, they love their gorges in upstate New York) in the Earth's crust was going to compare to roller coasters and cotton candy in Florida or California. Thanks for trying, Dad.

While my father's connection to religion may have been dubious, his connection to his native Pakistan was *tight*. And despite those allegedly empty pockets, he found a way to return there *every* year. He would leave Canada in mid-December, one day before the price of international flights peaked, and we wouldn't see him again until the third week of January, when he would return to work as the most jet-lagged person on the college campus.

My father would leave Canada with two massive suitcases—one packed with all his clothes, the other full of gifts for his siblings, cousins, nieces, and nephews. That second suitcase would then be refilled with gifts in Pakistan, destined for our family and other relatives who lived in Canada. And if my father was stopping in England on his way back, which was most often the case, that suitcase would also need to have some room in it for my father's mandatory purchases of shirts, sweaters, pyjamas, and/or a housecoat from Marks & Spencer. My father would also head to Pakistan with a handbag that was jam-packed with his sixty-plus students' final exam booklets (and hopefully a toothbrush). He would mark each one of those exams on the flight, and then pay exorbitant fees—in the pre-internet days—to mail the marked booklets back to his college. It was all a very exact science. But the point was, come hell or high water, he was *going* to Pakistan. The rest of us would go every ten to fifteen years or so.

At age fifteen, after a personal twelve-year hiatus, I was informed by my mother that we were all going to Pakistan. We were to go visit my father—who, if you recall, was on his sabbatical from Canada—in Saudi Arabia, and then as a family, we would all head to Pakistan. A voyage, in a plane, across oceans, to meet loving relatives and curious cousins—I was kind of excited. At sixteen, although I was starting to come to terms with my failures in the religious arena, I was getting more curious about my culture. This was a marked shift in my attitude. Had my parents told me even two years prior that we were going to Pakistan, the conversation would have gone like this:

> **Dad:** We're going to Pakistan!
> **Me:** Why?
> **Dad:** We want you to see where you're from.
> **Me:** But I'm Canadian. I'm from here.
> **Dad** (*to Mom*): Do you want to tell him or should I?
> **Mom:** You're Pakistani.
> **Me:** Pfff. You're crazy.

I'm paraphrasing, but at that age, that absolutely would have been my sentiment. My level of denial was pretty incredible: "At my very essence, I'm Canadian! I'm a white, Canadian kid. A white Canadian kid who eats kebabs, naan, and mint chutney for dinner, has about fifty Brown family friends, goes for Eid prayers, understands Urdu and Punjabi, and goes to Islamic Sunday school every week. You know, a white kid! *Why is this so hard to understand?*"

But fifteen-year-old me was intrigued. (Also, any suggestion that I might be okay on my own at home for three weeks was going to be squashed very quickly. I was intrigued, *and* I had no other options.) We had a total of twenty-one days of vacation to play with. On paper, four days in Saudi Arabia and seventeen in Pakistan seemed like the perfect mix. But we were completely ignorant about the aforementioned work ethic of the Saudi exit visa office employees. The trip wound up being a full two weeks in Saudi Arabia and one week in Pakistan. Yet another reason to look upon Saudi Arabia with great disdain.

Our flight out of Saudi Arabia to Lahore, Pakistan, was a memorable one, and not just because we were desperately anxious to finally get the hell out of that country. It is emblazoned in my memories forever, because on that PIA (Pakistan International Airlines) flight, we were served the most unique breakfast meal. It arrived covered in foil and I expected a basic oatmeal or, if we were "lucky," a hard-boiled egg and a bread roll. My only memory of a flight prior to this one was from Montreal to Indianapolis, but I had already learned to somehow manage my expectations of airlines. I opened the breakfast tray, and to my complete amazement, there lay a spicy omelette accompanied by two *shami kebabs*! Shami kebabs are tender, round patties made of ground meat, split peas, spices, and herbs. They are dipped in an egg mixture and pan-fried, and—if you'll allow the overly Canadian unit of measure—they are half the thickness and two-thirds the diameter of a hockey puck. And they are delicious. Typically, at home we had shami kebabs as a special treat, like if out-of-town guests were coming over. Mom wasn't going to hand-grind meat and lentils for just any old schlub (i.e., her son). But here was this airline, serving me shami kebabs that rivalled the best any aunty had ever fed me, *for breakfast*, like it was no big deal. And it occurred to me in that moment that PIA was, without a doubt, the absolute best. (Spoiler alert: It turns out that, in fact, PIA may not technically have been "the absolute best." In 2020, PIA was actually banned from flying in European airspace for six months after it was determined that the airline was "not capable of certifying and overseeing its operators and aircraft in accordance with applicable international standards.")

There is one good thing I can say about Saudi Arabia: it certainly is a good dress rehearsal for Pakistan. Saudi Arabia has a lot of dust, a lot of noise, and a lot of Brown Muslim people. Pakistan is all that, times ten. When I stepped out of the airport in Lahore for the first time, it was an indescribable chaos. People were yelling, scrambling, directing, honking. And the concept of personal space, as I understood it, was a thing of the past (although, keep in mind that the most jostling in a crowd I had seen up to that point was in the front row of a Huey Lewis and the News concert).

My father's youngest brother, Mana Chacha, was standing outside the airport to greet us, and I couldn't have been happier to see a friendly face. He also looked a lot like my dad, so it was an oddly familiar face. As we approached him, a small man came by, grabbed my suitcase right out of my hand, and started walking to the curb with it! My uncle quickly walked up behind him and snatched it back. I remember thinking, *Is that it? Shouldn't we also kick that guy's ass?* My uncle explained with a laugh, "Oh, he's just a cab driver, trying to get your business." What the hell? That was a sales tactic? First lesson in Pakistan: Things that could get you arrested in Canada might just be sources of amusement in Pakistan.

If you've travelled the world, you'll know that Pakistan wasn't really "chaotic." For locals, it simply operated differently. In a city concentrated with four million people (now nearly fourteen million!), where many roads are unmarked and all were shared by cars, jeeps, vans, buses, scooters, mopeds, rickshaws, cyclists, and animals, the rules and norms obviously have to be different.

My father is the eldest son in a family of nine children. The eldest son in a South Asian family is always afforded an inordinate amount of respect, and my dad was no exception. Even though he visited every year, they made a huge deal about it. The extended family catered to his every wish and whim. They gave him space when he needed it and hovered over him and smothered him with attention at all other times. Any food he was craving, any place he was thinking of visiting—it was as good as done. It was bizarre to see my fifty-something-year-old father getting spoiled rotten. And it seemed grossly unfair that this treatment be afforded only to male offspring. And unfair though it may have been, I—the eldest boy of the eldest boy—was also keen to get some of that treatment. That's . . . not exactly how things went.

Many of my aunts and uncles did shower me with love. In fact, it still warms me to think about how people whom I had no recollection of ever having met could be so warm and loving. My cousins, on the other hand, were a different story. It's more accurate to say that they approached me the way you might approach a gorilla in a zoo. *Hey, look—he makes noises, but they don't sound like ours. He moves his arms differently when he throws a ball. His hair is business in the front and party in the back.*

Even before leaving Canada, I was already rehearsing so that I would fit in with my Pakistani relatives. I would sit in my room, stare at the wall, and practise words with particularly difficult pronunciations. *"Ulloo ka pattha. Ulloo ka PATTHA. ULLOO KA PAT-THAA!"* It means, literally, "son of an owl," which is as bad a term as "son of a bitch," and an odd and inappropriate choice of words for a fifteen-year-old to be practising before going to visit relatives, except that the hard *t* in *pattha* required a hell of a lot of practise. *If I can just nail that down, I'm as good as gold,* I surmised. As soon as I met my cousins, it became abundantly clear that all my practise and effort didn't count for a damned thing. My Urdu-Punjabi hybrid with a Canadian accent turned out to be a great, unintended source of comedy. And as is the case with so many languages, the exact pronunciation of a word is often critical. For example, in Punjabi, the word *kora*—depending on how you pronounce it—could mean "bitter" or a "horse" or a "whip"! Clearly, when I was trying to explain that "my malaria pills taste bitter," there was some great comedic potential afoot. As soon as I spoke, no matter what I was saying, cousins would look at each other and suppress a laugh. Or just laugh at me directly. They were behaving like some real *ulloo ka patthas*, to be honest. The thing is, my own father—a product of this same environment—had been making fun of my accent for years. I really should have been emotionally prepared for this moment. But I had hoped for more from family members who were my own age.

During one impromptu game of cricket, I remember tossing the bat aside after I made a hit. This somehow turned into the most hysterical thing my cousins had ever seen. In baseball, you don't run with the bat; it turns out in cricket you do. Relatives were doubled over, bellies were held, fingers were pointed, tears of laughter were shed. *Hey, where's all the spoiling?* Well, at least they weren't focused on my accent for a little while.

And it wasn't *just* my cousins. After all, they learned the teasing from somewhere. One late afternoon in Lahore, as we were all gathered in an uncle's driveway preparing to leave his house, he offered my little sister a candy. Then, just before placing it in her hand, he "made it disappear." Suddenly, he was deep in character, acting completely dumbfounded about where the candy could have possibly gone. He actually hugged us all goodbye, let us get in the car, and just as we were driving off and the car was in motion, he revealed that the candy had been in his hand the whole time. My sister started bawling. We continued driving and I looked back to see him laughing his ass off.

Let's recap: A sixty-something-year-old man offered a candy to a kid, hid it, made her cry, *still* never gave it to her, and laughed hysterically at the "fun" of it all. What fresh hell was this? They called it "teasing." In Urdu, it's called *tang karna*, which translates directly to "bothering someone." For some of my relatives—and keep in mind that this could be unique to just my family—*tang karna* was a full-time occupation.

In addition to the teasing, there was another habit my cousins had to which I was not accustomed. It turned out that my family was universally regarded as rich. RICH? My administrative assistant mom and my frequently penniless, chronically in-debt father? *HA!* I said to myself. But because of this perceived wealth and a tradition (that I did NOT know about) of older cousins being expected to treat their younger cousins to anything they want, I found myself in some awkward situations.

"I like your shirt, Ali Bhai."
"Yeah, it is pretty nice. Thank you."
"No, Ali Bhai, I *really* like your shirt."
"Again, thank you."
"I really, really like your shirt."
"It feels like . . . you want my shirt."
"Oh! Thank you, Ali Bhai!"
"Dad, these people are taking the clothes off my back!"

My dad would immediately reassure me, "Don't worry, don't worry. We'll buy you more shirts at home." I was concerned that the man who turned his pockets inside out to show me how broke he was might not in fact be able to deliver on that promise. It felt like some bizarro version of a "What happens in

Vegas, stays in Vegas" situation, except Vegas was Pakistan and the only strip-per was me—giving my clothes to my cousins. And *my father* was the one who wasn't going to remember any of it. At one point, a cousin of mine even started eyeing my Montreal Canadiens jersey. Come on man, it's a signed jersey! And you don't even know who Mats Näslund is! (It turns out that *lund* means "penis" in Punjabi, which may have accounted for some of the looks I was getting.)

For our relatives, the concept was simple: My dad had emigrated from Pakistan to Canada, and he was a professor. Ergo, wealthy. And certainly, he *was* much better off than his working-class siblings and relatives. But what the hell did I have to do with that? I was a teenager! Oh, *now* you want to treat me like I'm my father's son?

Amid all the mockery and blatant disregard of my attachment to my own clothing, there was one bright spot. In the back courtyard of my aunt's home, chained to the wall, was a pet goat. I never had a pet of any kind, never mind a goat. ("You want a pet? We'll take you to the zoo!" was, if I recall, the Hassan family solution.) This animal was a nervous little guy, too, but for some inexpli-cable reason he became calm around me. He would stop quivering and lick the palm of my hand. He made *me* feel wanted. He probably thought my cousins were abusive jerks, too. Amidst the humiliation I was suffering from my relatives, time spent with this goat was my safe haven. In retrospect, it feels like we might have been providing each other with a kind of therapy. We spent so much time together in the first three days of that visit that I even named him: Billy. Not super creative, I know, but if it helps, we can pretend it was short for Bilal.

One day, I came to the backyard to find that Billy was gone! His chain was still there on the ground of the courtyard, but the little bugger had made a run for it—without me! I was devastated. I ran to my aunt, hopeful that she could provide some clues about Billy's disappearance, but she changed the sub-ject quickly and went back to stirring the contents of a large pot on the stove. Probably too bewildered by the news of Billy's escape to even talk, I figured.

The next obvious suspects were some of my cousins. These professional teasers might have taken Billy to a field and rode around on him like a horse. But I saw them around the house, and Billy wasn't with them.

That night, at a big family dinner, I must have been sulking, and an uncle—one of these rough-around-the-edges characters—asked me if I was enjoying my time in Pakistan. *No*, I wasn't. "No? Why not?" he bellowed. Because Billy left! "Billy?" he said. *"Billy is on your plate! Hahahahahhah!"*

Have you ever been told, mid-bite, that you're eating a friend? It sucks. Turns out that goat wasn't a pet in a courtyard. He was dinner in a holding pen. Pakistan, you cut me deep. And yes, I really should have picked up on all this earlier, but I didn't.

There were some genuinely lovely moments in Pakistan, but I was developing a knack for ruining those, as well. On the day that we were scheduled to leave Pakistan to come back to Canada, we visited one of my father's sisters. Her family wasn't particularly well-off, financially, but she was kind enough to buy me a gift. I opened it in front of her, and a number of other relatives, as they requested.

It was a gift-wrapped small wooden box with a nice design on it—the kind of thing that could hold a few nice pens or a necklace inside it. In my entitled Canadian existence, I had never received a box as a gift. Boxes were what held actual gifts inside them, right? I mean, what the hell did I know about Pakistani woodworking! While my various aunts and cousins looked on, I opened the wrapping, and said out loud, "Oh, it's a box!" as a joke, to suggest the idea that *Imagine if someone gave you just a box? LOL.* I opened it up to reveal nothing inside. You idiot, it *is* just a box! I had made fun of the gift directly to and in front of the people who gave it to me. My stomach turned, I closed the box, and looked up: "Thank you, Aunty, I love it," I said, hoping my face wasn't too deep a shade of maroon.

Later that day, as I sat in my shame at a family friend's home waiting for a large taxi to arrive to take us to the airport, a cousin of mine ran into the house, relieved to see that we hadn't left yet. He was a sweaty mess—he had just ridden his bike through unbearable Lahore heat and traffic to bring me a gift. He also wanted me to open it in front of him. It's a thing my family seems to enjoy. It was a gift-wrapped can of shaving cream. A North American brand, too. Now, I had access to shaving cream in Canada. He even likely knew that I had access to shaving cream in Canada. But that gesture—a thirteen-year-old buying me something with his own money (of which he would have had quite little) and racing it over to me in thirty-five-degree weather, meant so much to me and taught me something very valuable about the generosity of Pakistanis. Sure, some of them may want the shirt off your back, but it's because they themselves have so little. And yet despite having so little, they'll go to great lengths just to make sure they can present you with a gift.

At some level I knew this: No amount of Mötley Crüe's *Shout at the Devil* or downhill skiing or visiting cottages could alter the fact that I was a Pakistani. I would never have been so disgusted with my reaction to that box, or so touched by my cousin's gift, had I not felt this. I just wasn't ready to come to terms with all of that just yet.

My short time in Pakistan left me feeling hollow. Truthfully, I didn't "get" the Pakistan that I saw. And I didn't feel worthy of being Pakistani. Jokes, when I wasn't the subject of them, were lost on me. I couldn't recognize a goat that was destined for slaughter. I couldn't recognize a thoughtful Pakistani gift. And back home (Canada), I had already started to become a jack-of-all-cultures, which only confused things further.

For better or worse, my children have been spared all of this. We might actually be going too far in the opposite direction, in fact. Any time we've had money for a trip, we've thought of all kinds of destinations, except Pakistan! Once, when our family arrived at a resort in Jamaica, I watched my then three-year-old sit on a chair on our balcony overlooking the beach (a view I paid extra for), put his arms behind his head, and let out a sigh of boredom. I was in disbelief. I wanted to grab the kid by the shoulders and say, "Hey, we're in Jamaica, you dingdong! My father went on trips without me all the time, took me to Ausable Chasm once, and hugged me twice in my entire life. Do you understand how good you have it?!"

One day I'll take all my kids to Pakistan. They'll see what true love and generosity look like, and most important, what real struggle looks like. My hope is that it will encourage them to be grateful for what they have. But who knows, if they're anything like me, it might backfire and completely muddy their concept of identity.

Chapter 9

HONORARY EVERYTHING

IN MY LAST YEAR of high school, recently dismayed by my lack of authenticity as a Pakistani on our family trip, I started to drift away from all things Pakistani. It would be easy to simply reflect on my youth as that of a kid who was Brown on the outside and white on the inside—a coconut, we used to say—but the truth was deeper than that. I was being introduced to new cultures and communities, and I found them exciting.

I mentioned my buddy Zach earlier, who was Parsi. His family would often take me with them to Parsi events. I was already at their house; they were going to these various functions; I didn't want to go back home; and they had a large station wagon. It sort of worked out organically. Before I knew it, after having attended over a dozen house parties, events, and functions, Zach's mom deemed me to be an "honorary Parsi." And I liked it.

By the way, I might have seamlessly become an honorary South Indian, too, courtesy of my friend Tom, except he was barely South Indian himself. This is the same kid who, when pressed, only knew one curse word in his native language, and it translated to egghead. And while South Indian Tom Mathai may have been the whitest friend we had, ironically his nickname was "Darkman"! And before you go thinking, *Kids are so cruel with their nicknames*, he gave *himself* that one! When Zach and Tom would stay over at my place, Tom—a merciless prankster—would crawl around in the darkness of my basement and suddenly appear beside one of our mattresses, revealing nothing but the whites of his eyes and saying, "Beware of the Darkman!" He was positioning himself as a creature *of* the dark, you see. And it would actually scare the crap out of us. But these days, publicly yelling, "Hey, Darkman, what do you want to order?" at a restaurant, to your visibly very dark-skinned friend . . . Well, let's just say that it's a nickname that didn't stand the test of time.

While there exists some incredible Pakistani and Punjabi music in the world—qawwali and bhangra are worth looking up if you don't know about them—I went deeper into my worlds of heavy metal and rap. A weird combo for sure, but that's what you get from a fella who doesn't quite know who he is. And to complicate matters, the girls I liked had other tastes. Olga Courtois likes Wham!? Well, I don't know if that sexy ladies' man George Michael would care for a *male* fan, but here I am! Mia DeMontigny likes Tears for Fears? Well, you know what, I'll trade in a few of my tears for those fears, too! Susan Groundwater is into Joy Division? Why, Sue, you should have told me earlier, I thought I was alone here! (By the way, Sue, if you're reading this, that band really sucked. *Joy* Division? That miserable group should have been sued a hundred times over for that bit of fraudulence.)

Despite those hours of practising Urdu to my bedroom wall, the language was now becoming a source of discomfort. Anytime my mother would speak Urdu in front of my friends I would quickly reply in a panicked "Mom, English!" concerned that my friends might think she was talking about them. Often, she *was* talking about them, but it was more in the vein of "Does Jeff want something to eat?"

And there was nothing that I was more hyperaware of than the smell of Pakistani food. The possibility of having that smell on my clothes was terrifying. I'll never forget the feeling of coming downstairs to the smell of my parents frying onions, garlic, ginger, and various spices and seeing our hallway closet open, even a crack. "No! NOOOO! Mom, we talked about this!" I'd have to run outside with my jean jacket in hand, and aggressively shake it into the wind before my friends came to pick me up in their Chevrolet Chevette. I mention the type of car because four guys in it was a snug fit, and five was downright uncomfortable, *especially* if one of you smelled like a fresh Pakistani curry. And you were definitely going to hear about it. Somebody was going to absolutely, confidently say the words: "Dude, you reek like curry." And there was no witty retort for that. No quick clapback. You had to sit in the sting of that heckle. You weren't going to be able to say, "Well, guys . . . research is showing that the turmeric in curry is actually proving to be quite effective in combating a number of diseases, including Alzheim—" SHUT UP, NERD! Firstly, that research hadn't come out yet. And secondly, teenagers in Montreal did not care about the health benefits of turmeric.

After high school, most Québécois students head to CEGEP, the two or three years of college education we receive before university. Dawson College, where both my parents worked, was one of these colleges. And there was one thing I knew about Dawson College—I sure as hell wasn't going to go there and be under the constant watchful eyes of my parents! I elected to go to a local college, close to home, called Champlain College.

My fellow classmates consisted of many people I'd gone to high school with, gone to Sunday school with, played volleyball against, and friends of friends with whom I'd grown up. Within weeks, my days at school consisted of skipping class, playing cards, smoking cigarettes, shooting pool, and sampling the regional fare (poutine) at neighbourhood diners. And despite all this time spent missing class and becoming a renaissance man, it will amaze you to hear that my marks were awful.

By the end of the semester, I had six courses that I nearly failed (or barely passed, depending on if you're a cup half-empty or half-full type of person), and one 90 percent . . . wait for it . . . in FITNESS. Even Fitness itself would have been mortified to find out I was getting a 90 in Fitness. I was primarily beer and gravy in those days, but who was I to argue with the one mark bringing my grade average up to a 62 percent.

No matter what activities I was involved with in high school, good or bad, I had always maintained good grades (chemistry and physics notwithstanding). This was a whole new feeling. And it was very troubling. Worried about my future for the first time in my life (it would happen again many, many times), I applied to transfer out of Champlain to a different institution—none other than the aforementioned Dawson College. Maybe Mom and Dad's watchful eyes could be of some benefit.

Dawson College was in downtown Montreal, so I had to cross a bridge from our hamlet on the South Shore of Montreal to get to it. And in so doing, I also crossed a metaphorical bridge into what was effectively a whole new world for me. It was like going from a family get-together to a convention centre. Suddenly, I met hundreds of people from a multitude of cultural backgrounds: Italians, Greeks, Métis, Latinos—and for some reason that I can't fully articulate, I became a magnet for Brown people of all stripes. And these weren't the Brown people hiding in plain sight that I was accustomed to, these were people who were both proud of and knowledgeable about their background. I was being invited to participate in South Asian students' association events; I was meeting and dating Brown women for the first time; and I started down a path of what eventually became kind of a "thing" for me: selling samosas.

My dad had become known as the "Samosa Man" at Dawson College faculty meetings. Now a little older, the faculty was having fewer smoke- and booze-filled house parties, and more faculty potluck dinners. My dad had ingeniously made his life very easy for these potlucks: he would drive ten minutes up the road from the college to a legendary Montreal Indian vegetarian institution called Pushap, and pick up a box of fifty samosas, for something like forty cents a samosa. And when he would arrive at the potluck, grease-lined box in hand, everyone would shout with an enthusiasm that you can't even imagine, "Samosa Man is here!" On paper, he was just a guy who was bringing outsourced greasy potato-stuffed dough to a party, but in practise Dad was always greeted like a hero at those potlucks. I imagined some poor faculty member, showing up to the dinners with their "famous garlic sour cream bread bowl" or generations-old "secret family recipe duck pâté," only to be ditched mid-description for samosas.

"Well, you see, I can't divulge much. My family would kill me. But
   the secret is in the type of wine you use as a poaching liq—"
"Hey! The Samosa Man is here! Excuse me, I'll be right back."

"Oh. Ahem. Anyway, I started the preparation for the duck in this recipe about three months ago, as I was about to tell your colleague. Until he ran off to get samosas—"

"What? The Samosa Man is here? Excuse me, I'll be right back."

"Dammit! Faruq Hassan and his stupid fried triangles. He didn't even make them himself!"

That *had* to have happened at least once at every single faculty meeting for thirty years.

Following in my dad's footsteps, I started down an inconceivably long path of being a purveyor of samosas. First, I started selling premade ones at fundraisers, and decades later I was making my own as a caterer. But that time at Dawson College is when "Little Samosa Man" was born. Just to be clear, it was the samosas that were little. The man was large and overweight. And getting fatter, given that I was commonly getting high on my own (samosa) supply.

After Dawson, I started at McGill University, and the local South Asians I had been associating with expanded to Brown people from coast to coast of Canada, parts of the US, the West Indies, the Middle East, and from all over South Asia. And so now I was hearing about the poetry of Rabindranath Tagore from my Bangladeshi friend, Shona (books of poetry my dad actually owned but which I had never opened); I was appreciating bhangra and qawwali music at a whole new level as my friend Sandy blasted both out of his car speakers; and I was bonding with my friend Arsalaan from Dubai about how poorly the Saudis and Emirati treat South Asians.

I was also meeting guys like my friend Ravi, from Jonquière, Quebec. When I told him how white my adolescence had been, he said, "Dude, what are you talking about? I grew up in Jonquière! Brown population of five! My dad, my mom, my brother, my sister, and me!" And my friend Dave, from Nova Scotia, but originally from Trinidad, with whom I bonded over the Montreal Expos, the writings of V. S. Naipaul, rum, hot sauce, and the significance of cricket for people in the British Commonwealth. Among all these great new people, I had found my tribe. My tribes, to be accurate. And when I say found, I mean I *immersed myself* in them all.

My friend Sandy started taking me to a Sikh religious gathering every Saturday evening that would take place in a makeshift temple in a community member's basement. It was called *kirtan*. Someone would play tabla, someone would play harmonium, and typically, someone with an obscenely beautiful voice would sing religious hymns. Now, I think it should be pretty clear by this point that there wasn't much religious left about me, but that music would relax me and take me to an almost meditative state. If I'd been able to sit cross-legged in those basement *kirtans*, I dare say that those nights might have even been a "spiritual" experience. In under a year's time, I was deemed an "honorary Sikh."

My Trinidadian friend Dave had introduced me to his parents, his grandmother, and all his family members, and I'd even gone to visit them outside Halifax. They ordained me an "honorary Trini," probably most of all because I kept going back for more pepper sauce (Scotch bonnet pepper, by the way, not the black stuff) on everything we'd eat together. I would sweat all over my then-bald head, my eyes would well up with tears, and Dave's father would even say, *"Why he eatin' it? Clearly, de boy like de peppah, but de peppah doh like him!"* But I'd keep plugging away at it. "Honorary Trini" might have even been bestowed upon me out of pity, but I felt like I earned it!

And thanks to my friend Karen, I was also given the title of "Honorary Goan." Goa, you may know, is an Indian province that was once colonized by the Portuguese. For that reason, its very Indian-looking people are also very much Catholic and will often have family names like D'Souza, Alonzo, Alfonso, De Mello, Pinto, and so on. It kinda blew my mind the first time I met them.

Karen made it known to her parents that I was alone at Christmas one year—my father had made his annual pilgrimage to Pakistan and my mother and sister were visiting my aunt in the US. I was in fact very happy to be alone at home, but Karen's parents were having none of it. "The poor boy is alone at Christmas!" I was Kevin in *Home Alone* before there was a Kevin. But as happy as I was to be alone, I was even happier to be invited to a Christmas party. And these were big affairs—seventy-five-ish people spanning four generations, tons of food, and lots of singing. And at that first party, and the many

I attended for years after, I wasn't just an "Honorary Goan"; I was an "Acting Goan"—deep in character! I was singing Christmas songs, backed up on guitar by Karen's (and now my) uncle Paul. I was helping to make and roll out desserts. I was handing out gifts. And I was diving headfirst into tons of delicious Goan food, including into a veritable Muslim nightmare, that even half of the Goans wouldn't eat, called sorpatel. It's a Goan delicacy, served especially if not exclusively at Christmas. It had the look of vindaloo (another Goan creation), but contained pork meat, pork liver, pork tongue, and—the way Karen's relatives made it—flavoured with this cashew liquor called *feni*, and cooked in vinegar and lots of red chilis. Booze and pork, together again! Over the years, my level of enjoyment of this dish has led to two separate reactions when the Goan uncles see me arrive at a Christmas party: either "Ali is here, break out the sorpatel!" or "Ali is here, *hide* the sorpatel!"

Zach's mom, Dave's mom, and even some Goan community members were all in touch with my mother one way or another over time—on the bus, in the grocery store, at other get-togethers—and they would all speak fondly of me and tell my mom how I was an honorary member of their community. I'm sure my mom smiled and thanked them for their kind words, but one day she came home absolutely furious and said to me: "I keep meeting all these people who say you're an honorary this and an honorary that. You're an honorary everything except Muslim Pakistani!" Touché, mother. Touché.

I tried to stay in touch with my Pakistani side. I really did. In my first semester at McGill, I attended the first meeting for the Pakistani Students' Association (PSA). At their inaugural meeting, an actual yelling match broke out over the subject of potluck nights. Half of the just (barely) formed organization wanted to make sure there could be alcohol at the potlucks, and the other half were enraged that the suggestion could even be made that an organization representing the Islamic Republic of Pakistan could ever dare to have alcohol at its events. Screaming and shouting ensued.

If a brand-new couple were to get into an aggressive fight on the first day they met, we'd make some assumptions about how that relationship is going to go. Using that logic, I quietly backed out of that room and never went back.

I pivoted quickly to a different student organization: the Indo-Canadian

Students Association (ICSA). At the ICSA, they were talking about things they wanted to plan for that upcoming semester: Bollywood movie nights (rated PG), visits to the *cabane à sucre*, ski trips, and samosa "bake" sales for fundraisers. I mean, these people were speaking my language!

The ICSA gave me a new sense of identity. I was no longer a white guy in my mind. I was a Brown man. Pakistani? Kind of! Muslim? Mmm . . . I still wasn't sure you could say that. But I was a pan–South Asian man of some kind, now interested in all the intersecting parts of the Brown world.

Chapter 10

WILD HORSEFLIES COULDN'T KEEP ME AWAY

AS I GET OLDER, I'm realizing more and more that everyone's love of something comes from somewhere. For example, my sister-in-law Amber loves brunch. Like, she takes her brunch *very* seriously. Don't be up late on a Saturday night flippantly talking about "doing brunch tomorrow" because that is a vitally important event, and she will be there. It seems innocuous enough. Brunch is social and delicious—it's very reasonable that she loves brunch.

But some further probing reveals that she loves it to this day because her family effectively denied her (and her siblings) the pleasure of a good brunch for most of their childhood. The family would often go on road trips across western Canada and the US. The visual that I have been given is that of my poor sister-in-law as a child, staring longingly out a motel room window, across the parking lot where a Denny's or Waffle House sat. She watched white people walk in and out of these quintessential institutions of brunch, and when she asked her parents if she could join them, the answer would always come back the same: "Brunch? Nonsense. We have bread and jam!" "Bread and jam" was so often the response that it eventually became one word: *breadnjam*. In fact, courtesy of my in-laws, it also became a verb: "Are we stopping somewhere or are we *breadnjamming* it?"

Before I became a cultural attaché to all communities, I was really just looking to be an "honorary white guy." But what does that even mean? And aren't most immigrants to North America trying to accomplish some of that, too? For me, it didn't mean eating canned salmon. It didn't mean buying the best-quality maple syrup. And unfortunately for me, it didn't mean immersing myself in the cultures and traditions of Indigenous peoples. It meant one thing above all else: the cottage. Whether you call it a cabin, a chalet, or a country home, it doesn't matter. I longed for it.

But when it came to fulfilling my childhood dream, my dad had his own version of *breadnjam*. Any time we asked if we could buy a cottage, my dad would respond, "Why? We can have a picnic!" It was just like the cottage, but without the insurance, the annual upkeep fees, or the traffic you're required to negotiate every bloody weekend. That's still my dad talking, in case you can't tell.

Admittedly, those Pakistani family picnics were fun. It was the pre-helicopter parenting and pre-sunscreen era—gangs of us kids would play and run around wild and unsupervised, stopping only to quickly shove some food in our mouths that had been grilled on a portable hibachi. Sure, the kebab burgers had more of a lighter fluid aroma than I would have liked, but there was no denying the fun.

BUT—the cottage. The cottage had a kitchen, a wood-burning stove, indoor bathrooms. In one case, when my father was lent a cottage from a colleague, it had a tennis court on the property! Above all else, for my young myopic brain, bolstered by the intense desire to belong, the cottage had status. To me, it meant you had made it as a Canadian. Without a cottage, *could we ever truly consider ourselves Canadians*?

Eventually, and without warning, Dad "graduated" from picnics to camping. Like, he fully bought into the camping. He purchased multiple sleeping bags, tents, propane tanks, and a kerosene lantern. He was craving a return to nature, conveniently ignoring the fact that he had never been *in* nature to begin with. For me, those camping trips quickly became the *breadnjam* of the cottage world. A fact that should quite rightly be regarded as ridiculous, because there are few things as *truly* Canadian as camping. This country is known for its great outdoors—what's more Canadian than honouring and celebrating those very outdoors! Be that as it may, even though I always wanted to "belong," camping was the line that made me go, "Ehh, I don't want to belong *that* much."

At the end of the day, I just don't enjoy being in the outdoors for extended periods of time. I sunburn (as I've mentioned), and on top of that the back of my bald head looks like a six-pack of hot dogs, which is very exciting for mosquitoes and other bugs. They come for the allure of cased sausage meat and stick around out of spite once they find out it's just my sweaty head. Also, I've just never been able to shake this thought: *Dad, you immigrated here decades ago from Pakistan, leaving behind your family, your friends, and your entire world. Did you do ALL that so your family could go shit in the woods two days a week?* I think we must have gone camping a grand total of six times before my dad gave up and called us all hopeless, but I feel like six times is enough times to know if you hate something.

Also, camping never felt safe! What the hell did this Pakistani immigrant family know about how to deal with snakes or wolves or, God forbid, bears? I have a number of camping-loving friends who have urged me not to worry about this because they take bear repellent on their trips. Or, you may know it by its sexier name: bear spray. The issue of course is that, either way you say it, the product still has the word "bear" in it. Think about this product for a moment. You're packing for your trip, you've got all your clothes and food, and then you say, "Hold on—forgot the bear spray!" You hold it in your hand, stare at the word "bear" that's clearly written on it, and then you toss it in your duffel bag and say, "Yup, gonna be a great little getaway." If I have to pack even a flyswatter for a weekend, I'm inclined to cancel that vacation.

And what if you *were* attacked by a bear? How does one, as a child of an immigrant, even have that conversation with their family?

"Holy crap—my son, what happened to you?!"
"Um, so I got mauled by a bear, Dad."
"Wow! Unbelievable. So, you're telling me a bear climbed up to the eleventh story of your downtown condominium, that your mother and I helped you put a down payment on, and mauled you?"
"Well, no, not exactly. We actually drove three hours north to a place that is known to sometimes . . . have bears. Basically, we

drove to the bear's home. We ate food that bears probably love. We sang songs that bears probably hate. And yet, inexplicably, I got attacked by a bear."

At that point, *most* immigrant dads are looking to finish the job that the bear started. I never had to worry about any such conversation, of course, because my dad would have been right there beside me in the campsite with some kind of misguided positive messaging, like "The bear just wants to smell us, eat our peanut butter, and leave!"

But the cottage was a different story. The first time I heard about someone owning a cottage, I remember being completely flabbergasted by the notion. A second home? My father and mother both worked tirelessly and could barely afford our one home! Second homes sounded like something that belonged to the lavishly, obscenely wealthy—people featured on the show *Lifestyles of the Rich and Famous*. And that's what made our first two cottage visits slightly more painful: both were owned by colleagues of my dad's. Fellow teachers! Doug Rollins, who taught jazz history at Dawson College, owned the first cottage we ever rented. And my dad's colleague Friedl—a Spanish teacher at Dawson, whose husband was also a teacher at Dawson, and *who were also both immigrants to Canada*—owned the second one! What a cruel realization that was: my father was making perfectly good cottage money and squandering it all.

Ignoring Friedl for a moment, I generally believed "the cottage" to be the place where white people went, for two measly days a week, to get *away* from ethnic people. If you disagree with that, you haven't been to one. But I know this, I accept this, white people have confirmed this—and so when I'm invited, I cherish it. In July 2019, I was invited to my friend Jeff's cottage. I drove about three hours to a driveway that ended on a lake, where I was met by a boat captained by Jeff. We boated . . . or would it be sailed? Coasted? Look, this isn't my area of expertise. In any case, we took the boat across the water to the small private island that houses his cottage. The outhouse notwithstanding, it was glorious. As soon as night fell, a group of friends sat by the water on the dock. A fire roared, we grilled, we ate, we drank—as one does.

At that point I was feeling pretty confident, like I'd "figured out" the cottage. It's a great place to relax, unwind, and, based on my limited experience, it's also the place where—at its core—white people go to brag about the type of chips they've brought. Every single guest, one after another, had some version of this:

"Guyyyys—Rippled All-Dressed!"
"Hold on, you gotta try the Sour Cream and Onion!"
"Buddy, the Ringolos are where it's at!"
"Wait! Ali, try the Ringolos *with* the Sour Cream and Onion!"

Yes, thank you, everyone, but they have these where I come from (Toronto)! Also, how were the corn chips getting more attention than the jerk chicken wings I made from *scratch*?

At one point in the evening, as the fire crackled at our feet, a creature of some kind landed on my skull. And I'm using the word "creature" because when something gouges a chunk out of the back of your head, "bug" or "insect" no longer apply. While we're on the subject, once you've added the word "horse" or "deer" to a bug's name, it should really be regarded as part of the animal kingdom, in my opinion. I felt a pain so sharp that I half expected to see a short person with a knife standing behind me. When I slapped and killed the creature, I got to see the size of it as it lay dead on the ground! For a second, I thought it was a small drone.

What I didn't realize, as I was basking in the confidence of my newfound killer instincts, was that apparently the amalgam of a fresh open wound, my sweat, and Ringolo fingers were a bad combination. When I woke up the next morning, there was a puck-sized swelling on the back of my head with a large scab in its centre. My ear ached, and my jaw couldn't open fully. Clearly, it was already time to leave the cottage.

And if you're a cottage owner, I know what you're thinking: *Did he try to wash it out with lake water?* Good Lord, yes, I tried your holy lake water, and it did not help. My friends act like a dip in the lake at the cottage will clear your acne, renew your soul, and cure your syphilis. (To be fair, I haven't personally tested any of those.)

The departure from the cottage was more embarrassing than it needed to be, too. I packed quietly and tried to not make a big deal about it, but the only way out of this place was via boat. Loud, motor-operated boat. Before I knew it, five other friends were down by the little beach area, sad and confused for me. I felt like I was being kicked off an episode of a show called *Cottage Survivor.*

Once back on the mainland (Toronto, again), it was time to get some answers. A pharmacist has always felt like a good first line of defence—they can spare you a trip to a doctor with a quick, easy analysis of your condition. I walked directly to the back of the drugstore, lined up under the rectangular board that says PRESCRIPTIONS, and told a pharmacist that I needed his help. I turned the back of my head toward him and asked, "What *is* this?" His eyes widened, he clutched the centre of his lab coat, and he half yelled, "EW, WHAT *IS* THAT!"

Okay, first of all, I came in here to ask *you* a question. Why are you answering my question with a question? Also, that was *my* question! And, what kind of pharmacist says, "EW"?! How about some professionalism, bud! I buy my Q-tips and hummus at this drugstore. Keep your voice down.

Clearly, I needed to see someone who could appease my concerns about my wound within soundproof confines. A visit to the doctor was in order. I went, I waited, I was seen. Diagnosis: *infection*. A SKULL INFECTION. Take a second with that. Most people do. I was on antibiotics for ten days and had a scar above my ear for three months, thanks to a "bug bite" at the cottage.

I have asked around since that day: no cottage goer or owner has *ever* heard of anyone getting a skull infection at the cottage. Originally, I had to wonder: Was this my lot for "stepping outside of my lane"? Had I "aimed above my pay grade"? Was I in fact not worthy of cottaging? But my own cooler head prevailed, and I realized quite simply that I had been putting too much pressure on myself. And the cottage.

The truth was, that cottage visit—prior to the "attack"—came easy to me. I didn't sunburn because there was a house in which I could periodically take shelter. No one required me to eat while sitting cross-legged or go through the horror of yoga. The entire time, I was in my element. Both Jeff and his wife,

Kyra, even told me after that trip that, my skull infection notwithstanding, I was "the perfect cottage guest." I cooked, I cleaned up after myself, I contributed. Not because I desperately needed to be invited back, either. Just because I was being myself.

I finally realized that the cottage wasn't the "be all and end all" that I made it out to be in my young life. That was all in my head. Or, outside on the back of my head, as it were. The cottage was just a *good time*. And if there is one thing I've always excelled at, it's having a good time.

Chapter 11

NO, I DON'T CARE FOR A DANCE

LET ME BACKPEDAL FOR A MOMENT: I don't *always* excel at having a good time.

Most of the places that I've been "dragged" to against my will have failed to extract any fun out of me. Sunday school comes to mind. So does camping. In life, you are forced periodically to accept who you are and are not. And a perfect example of that has been—would you believe—the strip bar.

I've always been someone who's curious about people's backgrounds—socioeconomic, home life, ethnic, ancestral, stories of immigration, what have you. I can't really say why, I just know that these things have always fascinated me and taught me so much about human nature.

But an exotic dancing establishment is where this curious mind is *not* welcome. Don't ask the dancers about anything personal. Don't talk to other patrons—men talking to men is bad for business. Just engage in a pantomime of phony conversations with women who view you as an obstacle between themselves and your money. And definitely don't talk to the owners.

> So, Vinnie . . . Can I call you Vinnie? Was this a business you dreamt about having as a child, or was it a family business? Did you develop the concept during business school? How do you manage your labour costs? Can one assume that the ladies are paid a fair wage? What's that? Security is here to escort me outside? Yes, that's probably for the best.

But honestly, the entire business plan is such a mystery to me. What if I just want to have a drink? *Yes, enjoy a thirteen-dollar bottle of beer.* What if I don't have cash on me? *No problem, there's an ATM in the club that charges triple the transaction fee you're used to paying.* Can I step out and make a phone call? *No in-and-out privileges!*

These establishments do succeed, of course, because customers see value in what they are spending money on: the nudity of strangers. Call me crazy, but this trifecta of loneliness, objectification, and corruption never aroused me. I'm someone who enjoys the nudity of someone I know, and ideally really like. The stories of love found at a strip bar were sad, tragic, and almost always a one-way street.

There *are* times, however, when a friend is a particular type of sad, and the only joy he can find in life is in the fake friendliness of a dancing woman. Or there are times when you have to go along with "the bachelor wants what the bachelor wants," and what he wants seems to be the company of a naked stranger (even though we all know it's the bachelor's friends who really need this). All that is to say, there are a number of times when I've been dragged to strip bars. Nearly every one of those times has not gone well.

Once, at an establishment near the airport, creatively named the Landing Strip, I was nursing a drink at the bar while my friend "charmed" strippers around the club. It was three in the afternoon. Just as my boredom was peaking, my friend yelled out to me: "Al! This woman is from France!" The sociologist in me was immediately piqued. Could this turn into an interesting conversation with someone from a different country? I walked over and excitedly said, *"D'où viens-tu?"* (Where are you from?) Silence. *"Est-ce ça fait longtemps que vous êtes ici en Canada?"* (Have you been in Canada for long?) No response. *"Est-ce que—"* She finally cut me off and growled, *"FINE, I'M ROMANIAN."* And then walked off in a huff, slightly angry and slightly embarrassed.

I wasn't mad. I didn't feel like I'd been lied to. In fact, had she stuck around after her admission, I would have told her the story of the similar plight faced by Bangladeshi and Pakistani restaurateurs, who often felt obliged to run "Indian restaurants" because their own backgrounds elicited feelings of unfamiliarity, or worse, discomfort from potential customers. A story that, I'm pretty sure, would have compelled her to leave anyway, so the point is moot.

Another time, at the end of a co-op work term, a colleague named Ilya offered to take me out on my last day of work. On paper, Ilya wasn't the type of person I would normally connect with. Computer savvy, tight with money, and fascinated with violence. He spent a lot of time talking to me about martial arts, knives, and other weapons like ninja stars and something called telescoping batons. My complete and utter ignorance about all those things never stopped him from talking about them. Which is odd. Imagine someone started talking to you about hockey and you said, "Oh, I've never had any interest in hockey in my entire life," and they replied, "Well, that's fine. Despite that, here's a constant barrage of information about hockey." That aside, he was kind, and exceedingly helpful in an IT department where God knows that I needed help. But as was the case with so many of my relationships, our real connection was over food.

When he offered to take me out on my last day, I assumed steakhouse, high-end sushi, or any one of a hundred terrific restaurants in Toronto. When he suggested the Brass Rail with a wry smile and I responded with a "What's that?" he was stunned. He informed me that it was a Toronto institution and even though I was a new-ish resident to the city, it was borderline offensive that I hadn't heard of it. My refrain about "Strip clubs aren't really my thing" was met with a "Hey, guys, Ali hasn't heard of the Brass Rail. I'm taking him there for his last day. Who's in?" Predictably, a good handful of guys were in.

We walked in there at 12:04 p.m. I found out there was a lunch buffet, but it remains one of the rare days in my life that I skipped lunch. I sat in the club, uncomfortable as always, pretending to enjoy myself. At one point, the DJ, with that stereotypical stripper-y DJ voice, got on the PA system: *Gentlemennnn— please put your hands together for the beautiful Jasminnnnnnnn.* I half-heartedly glanced at the stage and saw her. Jasmin, a beautiful Brown woman. *There were Brown strippers? When did this happen?* How *did this happen?*

To be fair, India probably has a bunch, but I'd never seen or heard of a South Asian stripper in Canada in the late nineties (believe me, word would have spread). Our culture was far too conservative for any of that. Who are this woman's parents? Do they know? What circumstances in her life led her to this vocation? Where did she grow up? As all of this was running through my head, Ilya elbowed me in the ribs.

"Wow, dude, I've never seen you look at anything other than food with that much interest."

"No, man, it's not that. I've just never seen a—"

"I'm getting you a lap dance."

As though she had super hearing for the words "lap dance," she was standing beside me in an instant. Ilya gave her the instructions and she pulled me away. I was clearly nervous as she led me by the hand to the dance booths. I guess it was *kind of* cute, in the way a thirteen-year-old getting kissed at his bar mitzvah might be cute. She started dancing for me, her butt slowly moving from side to side on my lap.

"So, what's your name?"

"Ali. What's your name?"

"Jasmin."

"Ah yes, I do recall hearing that."

"But my real name is Yasmin."

"No way! That's my mom's name!"

The room went very still in that moment. I'll never forget it. I also will never forget the look on her face—wondering why the hell I would bring up my mother at a moment like this. Coincidentally, I was wondering the exact same thing. She broke the tension with a very sweet smile.

"Do you want to start over?"

"Sure."

We talked for a few minutes more, but I probably came off sounding like a reporter with *Nosy Brown People Magazine* and we wrapped up before the song was over. I just wasn't ready for that moment. I wasn't mature enough to meet a Brown, Muslim stripper. It was like finding out Santa Claus didn't exist. Or DID exist. Not sure which analogy works best here. I guess it was like finding out Santa Claus exists, but he is a she, and she is a Brown stripper, and she's like, "Do you want your gift?" and you're like, "Forget the damn gift! I have so many questions!"

This might be hard to believe, but my strip bar visits did get worse than that. My friend Kash was going through a bitter divorce a number of years ago. There are, allegedly, amicable divorces, so I feel like the "bitter" isn't redundant here. Kash wasn't so lucky. He was desperate to forget about his domestic strife for a few hours, and the strip bar held the key to his temporary amnesia.

He had come to one of my comedy shows earlier in the night and lent a half dozen comedians the gift of his insane, contagious laugh for ninety minutes—and now it was my turn to return the favour. I tried to subtly suggest that we could have cheaper drinks at some other bar, but he quickly responded with something to the effect of "Drinks always taste better when your face is full of a woman's breasts." When subtlety failed, I tried to tell him that these places aren't really my thing, but this man was on a mission.

Kash walked into that basement club with a massive grin, almost giggling at the fact that there were only four customers in the place, total. I think he felt like it was our VIP night. Two topless women emerged from the back—a bouncer probably alerting them to the fact that their customer base had just increased by a third—and Kash elbowed me while simultaneously raising his eyebrows, thereby giving me the international sign for "Huh! Huuuhhhh!"

I looked at the women and, despite my best efforts, I could only think one thing, which I opted to say out loud for some reason. "I wonder if these girls had their father in their lives." Kash stared at me for a good seven seconds. That's actually a long time for two men to be looking at each other in a place where men aren't really meant to look at each other at all. Finally, he broke the silence: "You're right. You don't belong here." And we left.

When you're a wingman for a friend, it can involve some actual work. You have to be, or pretend to be, interested in any friends accompanying your buddy's object of affection. Sometimes you have to play along with whatever story he is telling. Sometimes you have to buy drinks. Being a wingman at a strip club, however, requires the least amount of effort conceivable from any man. Unfortunately for Kash, I couldn't even provide that. What he didn't know then was that I had already started dating my wife-to-be and was getting to know her daughters. Their biological dad was no hero, and I couldn't stop myself from wondering if my future stepdaughters might one day feel driven to the exotic-dancing industry.

Look—I had never been a dad, never mind a dad to daughters fresh out of their parents' messy divorce. And so that day, any fading hope to find "Ali Hassan, strip bar patron" officially died. He was now, at best, "Ali Hassan, strip bar research associate." And no one wants that guy around.

This may sound strange coming from someone who became a professional actor, but I just wasn't able to be something I wasn't. I've had to accept, over time, that there are some places I just don't belong. It's been a critical part of growing up and figuring out who I am. And in retrospect, it's actually been much easier than the other side of the coin: navigating who *other* people think I am.

Chapter 12

THE DAY I BECAME A MUSLIM

MY KIDS WILL OFTEN HEAR me reminisce about a period of my life when I lived in Chicago. Between the eating, drinking, live music, and the great friends I was making, it really was one of the happiest times of my life. And it contained one of my happiest days: it was Friday, September 7, 2001, the day I was laid off from my brain-numbing job as an IT consultant. It was also the Friday before 9/11.

I can guarantee that you've never met anyone happier to be laid off than I was. The only thing that grabbed my attention and retention less than Sunday school was IT. Which should sound completely demented coming from a guy who went $22,000 in debt to get a diploma to work in this field. Why *did* I become an IT consultant, then? Well, at a loss for what to do with my life, I looked around at my group of friends and asked myself: Who among this group isn't particularly smart, and yet making a decent living? There were quite a few. And what was that subgroup doing for work? The answer, overwhelmingly, was IT consulting. And so I reasoned that I, too, should become one of these, how do you say, IT consultants. It bears noting that this is probably the worst way to determine your life's path. It cost me a ton of money to find out that my friends are all pretty smart in their own way. In my defence, my friend Deepa once told me a story about how he had just gotten done with eating a garlicky souvlaki wrap, with extra tzatziki and onions, and his girlfriend kindly asked him to brush his teeth because they were going out to meet her friends. He replied, "Actually, you know what, I don't really want to. I like the flavour in my mouth right now." This resulted in a fight that almost ended their relationship. How was I supposed to know that *that* guy would be a savvy computer programmer and consultant?

Originally, I "knew" what I wanted to do. I wanted to be a chef. With my bachelor of arts in political science in hand, I told my mother this. Her reply was *"Bakwaas na karreya karr"* (Don't talk nonsense). When I told my father, he was just plain stunned. "Ali. In Pakistan, the cooks earn so little respect that people slap them on the back of the heads!" Okay, first of all, Pakistan needs to ask itself some hard questions about that type of behaviour. Second, I want to be a chef, not a "cook." And third, I want to be a chef in Montreal, not Pakistan, where those slaps will hopefully be replaced by *"Merci, Chef. Au revoir, Chef."* But in a family where academia was so prized, I wasn't going to get their blessings. More important, I wasn't going to get their co-signatures on the loan I'd need to help me get a culinary education. And so, I looked for something else. Sadly, what I settled on turned out to the biggest *bakwaas* of all.

IT was *always* going to be a horrible fit for me. The one computer class I took at university was a disaster. I had a great relationship with the Egyptian teacher, thanks to the many hours I spent in his office seeking extra help. We were so comfortable with each other that, once, when I asked him a question he felt I should have known the answer to, he yelled at me in front of the whole class in his thick Middle Eastern accent. "Ali, you fool! You still don't understand this?" It was Sunday school all over again. Except this time, I was kind of laughing at how hopeless I was. Most of the class was pretty horrified, though, I do remember that. My friend Salim asked me outright, "Yo, are you cool with that?" and there were a bunch of "He can't talk to you like that!" whispers after he yelled at me. I only made them more confused when I said, "Hey, it's okay. We're close!"

When I enrolled at the Information Technology Institute to finally pursue this ill-advised diploma, it only took a week before I was completely lost. My friend Q, who has notoriously never seen a challenge he wasn't up for, came from Montreal to Toronto on a train to tutor me. What an absolute sweetheart. And what a complete waste of his time. He spent eight hours trying to educate me, and when he was done the wall behind him looked just like the one in *It's Always Sunny in Philadelphia* when Charlie goes on a conspiratorial rant about "Pepe Silvia." (Look it up.)

That diploma program was eight months long, and every two months we would switch to a different module. First, we learned about the front interface of systems, and then we learned about the back-end systems, and then . . . and then I genuinely can't remember what we learned because of the aforementioned issues with my retention and interest. But for every module, we as a group had to decide what our project would be, and each time I would passionately champion for it to be food-related. "Let's build an online reservation system for a restaurant! Let's build a back-end inventory system for a restaurant supplier! Let's build a supply chain system for farm-to-producer-to-manufacturer-to-restaurant!"

I guess my passion was visible and my arguments were compelling, because one of my classmates, Winnie, even pulled me aside once to quietly scold me. "Ali, you don't belong in this program. When are you going to realize that your life belongs in the food industry?" Tell that to my parents, Winnie!

But, I somehow got through it and was hired to work at my first IT consulting job, over the phone by a wonderful man named Mark. Over the phone I sold Mark on *me*. I joked around with him in a way that I doubt any of his employees did. My guess is that Mark thought to himself, *This will be a great guy to have working for me. And the technical aspects of the job? Those can be learned once he gets here.* Very soon after I arrived in Chicago, Mark realized he was only half right.

Mark also sold me on the job. There were enticing promises of what was to come: "You ever been to Austin? *You're gonna love Austin!*" A week later, "Ali, things are moving fast here. It looks like we might need you in Raleigh, North Carolina, for a few weeks before Austin. But don't worry, the client is great and you're going to eat very well!" In reality, the tech bubble burst in the year 2000, about three weeks before I got to Chicago. My IT consulting life, which once held so much promise for travel, alternated between "working remotely" and "being on the bench"—both from a tiny cubicle in a nondescript building in a tech park in Deerfield, Illinois. For the next year and a half, I never even got to one client site. Austin remains an elusive travel destination all these years later. Raleigh can suck it.

I hated the work *and* I was terrible at my job. This is what's known as "a bad combo." And Mark, who had hired me, left to work for another company a month after I arrived. And I'm not exaggerating in the least about how bad I was—other South Asian employees would actually say to me, *"You should really quit this job, man."* Hey, don't we have a common background? A shared sense of community? A brotherhood? *"We do, but you're really bad at this. You should quit and go back to Canada."* Hold on—is someone from another country telling me to leave this country and go back to *my* country? What kind of multi-levelled discrimination *is this*?

Whatever it was, it was fair. I did not belong there. Every single one of my colleagues were obsessed with and excited by IT. *"Did you read about the new Palm Pilot in* Computerworld *magazine?"* Good God, no. Why would I do that? I would never even think to do that. But I *did* read about a new pressure cooker in *Food & Wine* magazine. Did you see that piece on Portland's rising food scene? What about Martha Stewart's blueberry crumble recipe? Anyone? *ANYONE?!* There was never anyone who had read what I had read.

I quickly became that guy who watched the clock every single day, waiting anxiously for lunch, and then praying to God for 5 p.m. as soon as lunch was over. (I guess praying *was* part of my life!)

And so, my layoff on 9/7 was a relief and a time to celebrate. I was elated. What a weekend 9/8 and 9/9 were. And my birthday was on 9/10! It's always on 9/10. It continues to be on 9/10. You know how birthdays work.

I'm not sure how common this practise is, but since my early twenties there are at least two times a year that I take stock of my life. On New Year's Day, and on my birthday. I think about the road travelled and the road ahead. I make goals for myself and look at what I've done, see what I can do better.

And as far as birthdays go, this was a big one. I had just been gifted a fresh start! The shackles of this miserable job and my associated miserable self were gone! As I lay there going through my biannual personal checks and balances, it hit me like a ton of bricks. I was going to make a change. No more IT consulting! No more sitting behind a desk and not understanding the first thing about what I was doing. I was going to make a break for it. I was going to get into . . . IT sales!

Okay, fine, so I was a little risk averse. Still, I was excited. I was going to update my résumé and get on all the job sites and start applying first thing in the morning. Tomorrow was going to be a great day!

As it turned out, "tomorrow"—or 9/11, if you prefer—was *not* a great day. It was maybe the worst day. We spent it calling our friends in New York, not knowing if they were alive or dead. Sure, I knew that my buddy Manny worked at Salomon Smith Barney, but where the hell were they headquartered? And even if they were uptown, what if he was at a client meeting in the towers that morning? The only people who knew where my friends in NYC worked were my other friends in NYC, and all the phone lines were down. It's not a day you wish on anyone. And if you remember that day, you may also recall that there was a missing plane that eventually went down in a field in Pennsylvania. But for a few hours, all that was known was that it was on a flight path in the direction of Chicago.

On the night of 9/11, my friends Deepa and Ravi and I headed out for a walk. We three Brown guys headed out, just to walk the streets and be in our community. After one of the most inhumane acts had taken place that morning, I think we just needed to be outside and a part of humanity. The streets were nearly abandoned, though, exactly as you might think they would be on 9/11. On Division Street, right behind my apartment, we walked past two men standing and chatting in a doorway. I gave one of them a nod. A truly unique nod, really, as if to say, "Hey, man, what a day, huh? Hope you're good. Who knows what the future holds after this. Hope we can all bounce back from this thing." All that, and more, in just a small movement of my neck and eyebrows. He didn't nod back, which was fine. Really. Chicago is an odd city sometimes—the Midwestern charm and kindness that its residents are known for exists also alongside some very macho, testosterone-fuelled, unfriendly men. Also, I didn't know what kind of day *he* had had. If he'd also had the worst day of his life, how could I expect him to respond to a friendly gesture that night?

As I was thinking all this and walking by him, he turned to his friend and said, "There go a couple of them right now."

It's sad that he said it, of course. But it's sadder still that I quite literally looked around and thought, *Who?* I actually walked a full block before it really settled in. When I tell this story, I'm often asked, "Why did it take you so long to realize those guys were talking about you?" Fair question. There was literally no one else on the street. A normal person might have picked up on that much earlier.

That night in Chicago, I honestly could have shrugged off any *"Hey, Paki"* or *"Go back where you came from."* I'm a Paki? Fine, you got four letters of it right and you're probably too stupid to know the history of that word, anyway. Go back where I came from? Fine, I hear New Brunswick is lovely this time of year. But that night in Chicago, that *"There go a couple of them right now"* . . . It cut me deep. We most certainly were not "one of them." But what we were, or what we wanted to be, didn't matter. Perception was reality. And the whole thing affected us doubly, in fact. I was worried about my friends possibly having been killed that day in New York City, and at the same time I was being accused of being just like those killers.

Maybe that night in Chicago, I was also slow on picking up the racism because I didn't want to hear it or believe it. After spending decades figuring out how to feel like you belong, in one instant you can be reminded that you don't belong after all.

Chapter 13

"GO BACK WHERE YOU CAME FROM"

THE TRUTH IS, I have always been slow on racism. Early on in my life, this made perfect sense: in my mind, I'd been a white guy until my mid-teens. I didn't look in the mirror every day, take a deep breath, and go, "Okay. Brown! Let's do this!" And when you see yourself generally as a white guy, you're bound to be a little slow picking up on racism. And I was.

One fine Saturday, at the age of sixteen, I found myself visiting my cousin in Cambridge, Ontario. Yes, we also have a Cambridge. No, it doesn't have a top-tier international university, but it has been described as a city with a "Dickens-like flair." Which I can confirm is quite the exaggeration; four square blocks have that flair, and the rest of the city seems to have a drinking and/or drug problem. My cousin Zaki from Chicago was also visiting during this time. As luck would have it, a girl in my cousin's class announced that her parents were going to be out of town and that she was going to throw a house party on Saturday night.

As the more seasoned partygoer of the three of us, I explained that, our religion and culture notwithstanding, bringing a bottle of booze to the party was simply good manners. My Cambridge cousin was fourteen, and my American cousin stood tall at about five foot four—so they both nervously looked to me to make this illicit purchase. I laughed in the face of their stress: "Of course I'll buy the booze, whaddya worried about!" My confidence was on account of the fact that I had been able to buy booze in my native Quebec for a number of years already. In those days, as long as your head was tall enough to peer over a gas station counter in *la belle province* and your arms could lift a case, and your mouth could say, *"C'est pour ma maman,"* you'd be all set.

We walked to the liquor store, and just as we pulled up to the parking lot, both my cousins ducked behind a garbage bin and mouthed, "Good luck" and gave me a thumbs-up. Good Lord, these amateurs! I walked into the LCBO, cool and determined, armed with some cash and my leather jacket. Having grown up in Quebec, I'd never been in an LCBO and had no idea what it stood for. If I'd been a betting man (boy) I would have figured "Liquor Consumption Beer Office" or some such thing. I clearly hadn't given it much thought. As I soon found out, courtesy of a large sign on the wall, it stood for the "Liquor Control Board of Ontario." I remember thinking to myself, *Control? Ha! Who could possibly control something as widely available to the general public as alcohol? What a terrible name.* Quebec had spoiled me rotten. As I strolled through the aisles, I saw more signs than I had never seen in all my years (2.75) of buying alcohol:

MUST HAVE A VALID ID

NO MINORS ALLOWED IN THE STORE

MUST BE 19+

Oh, okay. I'd been faking eighteen in Quebec, but this should be fine, right? What's another year to fake? I'll just lower my voice an octave. And then, one last sign: ANYONE CAUGHT WITH FAKE ID WILL BE PROSECUTED.

Now, it said "prosecuted"—which isn't good, by any means—but what I thought I was reading was "persecuted." I read it like I was going to be arrested and put on trial at a war crimes tribunal for acts of genocide. I'm still not sure why that final sign got to me. I didn't have a fake ID. I didn't even have any ID! But the aisles of the liquor store started to close in on me, and I could feel my breath getting heavy. I started to replay my cousins' reactions in my mind. No wonder they were nervous for me! I'd been taking this way too casually.

I picked up a bottle of booze quickly and made my way to the cashier. In line, I tried to control my breathing and imagined myself being asked for my ID. How would I handle it? I figured my best bet was to turn into Sam Elliott from the movie *Road House*, smile with a twinkle in my eye, and say, "Hang on a sec, darlin', I reckon it's just in my glove compartment." Yeah, that's what I'll do. Never mind that you need a car to have a glove compartment. Just say it, walk toward the exit, and then sprint like hell through those doors like the fugitive I was starting to feel like, and hope my cousins could keep up.

It was my turn at the cash register. I took a deep breath, hoping to portray even a shred of the confidence needed to make this purchase. The cashier glanced up at me, punched in the price of the bottle, and then said, "Fifteen dollars, please." Say what now? For a split second I was too stunned to move. I snapped out of it quickly and acted like it was NO BIG THING WHATSOEVER to be charged for the very bottle of booze you just brought to the register, took my change, and exited the store. It took me twenty steps to get to my cousins behind the garbage bin, and I held my breath for every one of them. "Are they behind me? Are they chasing me?" Once we were behind the store, we all cheered in relief. I removed the bottle from the paper bag to display my spoils of war. Oh, *shit*.

In my nervous haste, I'd picked up a one-litre bottle of Kahlúa. In case you're not familiar, Kahlúa is not exactly a "liquor," but a very sweet coffee-flavoured liqueur. It's most often added, by the tablespoon, to coffee, ice cream, and cakes. And even then, the world's most avid baker would need about five years to polish off a litre of Kahlúa. All three of us had raided enough friends' parents' liquor cabinets to know what a blunder this was. Essentially, I bought a large bottle of syrup. My cousins were both outraged, understandably.

"Guys! Beggars can't be choosers, all right? Look, I'm sorry, but I can't go back in there! Now, come on, let's all take a deep breath, head to the party, and start down our paths toward early onset diabetes, okay?"

And besides, for all we knew, there could be very enthusiastic fans of Kahlúa there and we could make friends with many young, sexy Cambridge, Ontario, ladies. Admittedly, that was a long shot. But we never even got close. After about an hour of walking through suburban neighbourhood streets, we got to my cousins' friends' house. The house was oddly quiet for one that was hosting a house party, and we were concerned that we might be the first ones there. Partygoer that I was, I also knew that this was a bit of a faux pas.

He rang the doorbell, and she came to the door quickly, but opened it just a crack. I never saw more than two and a half inches of her face. She whispered to us, "My parents didn't wind up going away! I'm sorry." I'll never forget my cousin's response: "Oh, okay, that's cool. We're cool." And with that, she shut the door. I would have described us as many things in that moment—embarrassed, thirsty, needing a sit-down—but certainly not cool. But when you're fourteen and facing that level of rejection, you have to do the ol' "Oh, we were just in the neighbourhood! And you were first on the list of various Saturday night parties we are hitting up. Sure, now we'll be getting to our second destination a little earlier than planned, but don't you even worry about that!"

If you were born after the year 2000, all this will make precisely zero sense to you. I get that. You're asking questions like "Why didn't she text him to say the party was off?" or "Couldn't she just send a mass email to everyone who was on the evite?" Oh, that would have been ideal, but you see, in the nineties—and all of time before that—there was no email. And more horrifying still, no cell phones. So, you just headed out to a house party on a Saturday night, assuming that nothing had changed since the invite to that party on Friday afternoon. And sometimes you headed out to that party on foot (because taxis were for big shots), and sometimes that party was a seven kilometre walk away.

We left her doorway and walked into the street. Well, more Kahlúa for us!—said no one, ever. But we did have a full bottle, and we did happen to spot many public parks on our walk over to the defunct house party, and we did now have some time on our hands.

Now, this chapter was intended to be about racism. In case you were wondering, none of the above qualified as such. The cashier at the LCBO, if anything, was now a hero to the local Brown community. My cousin's young lady friend—she was simply a victim of her parents' lack of commitment. When you say you're heading out of town, you head out of town! And the three of us? Thus far, we were simply the victims of the slow pace of phone technology, which hadn't caught up to the needs of young teens. And so, dear reader, I thank you for your patience.

We polished off the litre between the three of us, each giving up at different times, yelling, "I can't—it's too sweet!" and yet returning repeatedly with "Okay, one more sip." We headed back into the suburban streets for our long walk home, a syrupy coffee with notes of vanilla and alcohol emanating from our collective breath. Then, a sports car barrelled past us.

I should mention that, at this time, I was a huge Guns N' Roses fan. I had an *Appetite for Destruction* T-shirt, I had a GNR patch on the arm of my jean jacket, I had the long hair. God, there was so much hair. I get teary-eyed if I think about it for too long, so it's best to move on quickly. The point is, I was at peak Ali Hassan. Not one thing had started to spoil yet. And peak Ali Hassan loved his Guns N' Roses. At the time, they had a song called "One in a Million." There was a stanza in the song that started with the line "Immigrants and faggots." And wouldn't ya know it—a local Cambridge fella felt like he had found the opportune moment to recall that very line.

"IMMIGRANTS AND FAGGOTS!" he yelled into the silence of the night out of the passenger-side window as he sailed past us. I was a few feet ahead of my cousins, and didn't realize that my fourteen-year-old cousin picked up a large rock and whipped it toward the car. I would describe this, all things considered, as the correct reaction. As the rock just left my cousin's hand, I realized, *Hey, I know that song!* and began singing it, with a smile on my face.

". . . They make no sense to me. They come to our country, and think they'll do—" *Shit.* I realized then, as I watched the rock fall a few feet short of the car, just missing the back window, *that was racism.* The car continued to drive off. There was silence again. I turned back to look at both my cousins, hoping dearly that they hadn't heard me. No such luck. They were both completely dumbstruck.

"Dude. Did you think the guys in the Camaro wanted to have a drive-by duet with you?"

No, no. I'm just slow on racism.

There have been some moments when there was no mistaking what was happening, even for me. Something similar happened years later. In college, I once went to visit my friend Craig in London, Ontario. He was in law school and I was looking for a weekend of fun. We went to a house party in some fraternity that first night and had a great time. Our night ended at a 7-Eleven (they are open way past 11 p.m., in case you weren't aware) for some slushies and corner store sandwiches.

As we walked along the sidewalk of a main street, heading back to Craig's place with our arms full of goodies, a car full of young white dudes was stopped at a light beside us. One guy in the back seat rolled down his window. As soon as the light went green, he yelled, "Hey, Akbar, why don't you go back where you came from!" and they all cackled as they sped off.

I remember my own complete disbelief—I wasn't even in a group of Brown guys. It was me and my whitest friend. Scottish ancestry! A "ginger" for God's sake! I *still* couldn't get a pass? And I'll never forget Craig's absolute shame that this had happened. Shame for his town, or on behalf of the other white guys, I don't know, but it clearly stung him, too. And I remember this—still scarred from the Cambridge Camaro incident of years prior, I whipped my slushie at that car as hard as I could. Apparently also inspired by the Cambridge Camaro incident, I missed the car by a few feet. Now I had been told to go back where I came from, *and* I had no slushie. It was a long, silent walk back to Craig's place.

Blatant racism doesn't always present itself with so much anger, but that doesn't make it any less stunning. As a fully grown adult, in an audition for a film, I was asked by a casting assistant, "The production is looking for authentic casting for this cab driver—so, Ali, are you Paki?" That was . . . unexpected, but I told them I was in fact "of Pakistani heritage," hoping they'd get the hint.

Oddly, whatever negative emotions that question conjured up inside me helped me that day—I got a callback for a second audition. A producer was present and I remember thinking, *Ah good, a decent, informed, well-travelled member of society. This will be much smoother.* About three seconds after I had that thought, he asked me, "So, do you speak Paki?" COME ON, PEOPLE! I know that this all falls under cluelessness more than overt racism, but for the love of God, read a book. Learn something. Be better.

I'm sure that for a lot of people, that word doesn't seem so bad, but a short history lesson for anyone who has casually been asking people if they are Paki: In England, where the word was "ingeniously" crafted in the 1950s and '60s, it was effectively the N-word for Brown people. Indians and Pakistanis had been sent for by their recent colonizer to help build England into the place it is today. As a thanks, they were made to feel unwelcome on a regular basis. The word was not said casually in audition rooms, it was uttered through gritted teeth with venom and bile spewing out of a white person's mouth, preceded almost always with a "fookin'" or "dirty" (or both). I'm one generation under the people for whom it was their N-word. And when you know the history of the word, and when your father was called a Paki in England when he lived there, it's not always easy to just shrug it off.

There was another time I was immediately aware of racism, and it was an important, life-changing moment. It was also, oddly, exactly what I needed to hear. In the aftermath of 9/11, I was in the unfortunate position of needing work so that my US visa could be renewed. There weren't a lot of job openings then to begin with, and the hiring that *was* happening was mostly in IT security—which I had no knowledge of. It felt desperately tone-deaf to reach out to any HR departments in those devastating weeks, saying, "Howdy! These are my strengths and weaknesses and here is how I could be an asset to your company!"

In early November 2001, two months after 9/11 and with two months of unemployment under my belt, I was invited to a barbeque at my friend Anjuli's place. If you know about the weather in Chicago in November, you'll know that we gathered around that grill more for warmth than sausages that day.

Anjuli was flipping meat on the BBQ and making introductions between her seven or eight guests; she introduced a "Sunil" to someone, saying that he ran an IT firm. *What's that now?* What incredible luck! I scooted over to Sunil and introduced myself immediately. I told him that I had been working as an IT consultant but it "hadn't really been my thing" (I left out the sordid details). I told him I was looking for work in IT sales. The interaction that followed will stay with me forever.

    Sunil: What did you say your name was again?
    Me: Ali. Ali Hassan.
    Sunil: Yeah . . . Well, I wouldn't hire you.

As Canadians, we tend to forget about that jarring American honesty. I stood there for what felt like five minutes, staring at Sunil, confused and waiting for him to add, "Hahahah, just kidding, man! Wow, you should have seen your face. But seriously, come by my office Monday morning." No such luck.

He explained himself—probably to get me to stop staring at him with my dumb, hopeful grin. "No offence at all, but I have customers in Idaho, in Nebraska, in Ohio. They don't want to see an 'Ali Hassan' come into their office right now. And I don't know when they will."

To many, when I tell this story, Sunil sounds like the world's biggest asshole. I always want to see the best in people, and even I thought that, too, for about a day. But then I realized what a favour he had done for me. He'd told me exactly, in no uncertain terms, what the state of the American psyche was. He had left me with no room to fool myself or hope for the best. And most of all, he helped me realize that it was time to go back home to Canada.

Part 4

FOLLOW YOUR PASSIONS

Chapter 14

THEY'RE ALL GOING TO LAUGH AT YOU

IT WAS BECOMING CLEARER THAT I wasn't going to have much of a future in the United States post-9/11. But while I came to terms with that, I needed money—the bacon wasn't going to buy itself! The effectively closed job market and my paralysis when it came to sending out my résumé meant that I had to explore blue-collar, under-the-table work.

Someone referred me to a ragtag crew that was hired to do menial construction work for $100 per day. I had never been a snob about working. In fact, after a year and half in an ivory consulting tower, I relished the opportunity to join this hands-on assignment. It was time to do some real work! Real work wound up looking like this: I'd wake up at 4:30 a.m., meet a crew of Irish and Kiwi strangers in a van at 5, and head to an abandoned factory in which I spent ten hours assembling storage lockers and units. In a nutshell, I lifted and held up sheet metal while someone else (thankfully) drilled it together.

I worked for about a month, enthusiastically, until one day I had to ask myself, "Is sheet metal work really in my bones?" The answer was almost a yes when I dropped a heavy metal sheet on my own forearm and sliced my skin just shallow enough to not need stitches. I couldn't help but be reminded of my father's story of laying down tracks for the railway in Leeds. He lasted a few weeks; I lasted a few months. Hey, no one's trying to be a hero here! That hard labour, combined with a fellow Brown man's "I wouldn't hire you" comment still ringing in my ears, meant that it was really time to go. A few days before Christmas 2001, I loaded all my belongings into a Taurus wagon and drove back home to Canada. (By the way, if you're in your thirties and can load your *entire* life into a Taurus wagon, it's a good indication that you've made some mistakes.)

I came back with a renewed energy. First things first, I had to complete an MBA program that I had begun years prior. That's right, you read correctly: an MBA program. Sheet metal work wasn't in my bones, but wasting time and money certainly was.

Originally, I had enrolled in this MBA program for my dad, if I'm being honest. I wanted to make the "A bachelor's degree is nothing!" guy happy.

When you do something that you're not interested in, for someone else, it can be pretty difficult to complete. On that first attempt, halfway through my degree, my pitiful marks had become a blemish on the university. I was encouraged (read: required) to pursue something else. They weren't rude about it—they *did* wish me good luck with my "future endeavours." Maybe that's why getting laid off from work felt so natural—I'd already been laid off by a *school* a few years prior.

As you already know, my future endeavour was to become the world's worst IT consultant. But after my pseudo-voluntary exit from the United States, I was permitted to re-enter the MBA program, as long as I maintained an A– average. I guess that was fair, but this time I was more of an asset in class than a liability, thanks to the fact that I was one of the very few students with actual work experience: selling video equipment at Future Shop *and* consulting in the IT world. They didn't know I was a mediocre salesman and a terrible consultant, and they didn't *need* to know! Some days it felt like I was the only one with any intelligent questions. Me! Intelligent questions!

The MBA program was at McMaster University in Hamilton, Ontario. One of my most vivid memories of the whole experience was from my very first week, when I started the program the first time. All ninety of us brand-new students were corralled into an auditorium for a presentation by a certain Professor Marvin Ryder. I never saw him again, but I'll never forget his name.

He started our session thusly: "Put away your laptops and books. There won't be any notes." This caused an audible discomfort among my new class-mates, which confused me. *My* only thought was *No note-taking? Amazing! I like this guy's style.* He continued. "I want to ask you one question. How many of you, if money was no object, would be here today?" I almost laughed out loud at the thought, until I watched 90 percent of my classmates lift their hands.

WHAT? You have a million dollars and you're still going to do a co-op MBA in Hamilton, Ontario? Good Lord, did brown-nosing have no limits? (It's worthwhile to note that at the time I thought one million dollars was the equivalent of money being no object.)

I proudly kept my hand down as Mr. Ryder surveyed the scene. That pride dissolved instantly as he followed up: "Great, I want to talk to those of you who didn't raise your hand." Dammit. I hadn't counted on that. He panned across the room and looked at the eight or so of us who had some semblance of standards. He began with a girl closest to the aisle. "You, young lady—what would you be doing if money was no object?"

"Well, I live in Toronto, where there is a pretty serious homelessness prob-lem. I'd probably work with a shelter, helping get people off the street."

Crap. I couldn't follow that!

He worked his way in from the aisle, which meant he was going to ask me *very* soon. First, he asked another student, "What about *you*, young lady?" This woman also gave some selfless answer about building wells and bringing fresh water to African communities that made me sink in my seat.

He looked up at me, seated in the back row. "And yourself?"

"Well, sir . . . ummm . . . to be honest, I would be an actor, or a chef."

Mr. Ryder paused, addressed the entire class, and said, "Well, ladies and gentlemen, welcome the Fresh Chef of Bel-Air to our MBA program!"

It may go without saying, but a TV show called *The Fresh Prince of Bel-Air* was big at that time and the joke did *very* well in the room. He laughed out loud, and it turned out that I did *not* like this guy's style. Everyone in the audi-torium looked back at me and laughed, too. And as they turned back around, I muttered "F off" to the whole lot of them. Who were they to judge my dreams? I would have *loved* to have become a chef or an actor. What's wrong with that? The truth is, I actually would have added "comedian," too—because that *was* the truth—but one doesn't want to seem too unfocussed in all these dreams that one isn't pursuing.

Looking back now, it's amazing to me that I actually returned years later to finish the MBA. But I did complete the program. To be accurate, I completed the courses required for the program—but with "only" a B+ average. Let's be honest, that A– target was a long shot to begin with.

To recap: I was asked to leave an MBA program midway through, I barely completed an IT diploma program, I was a failed IT consultant who was *also*, it turns out, never going to hold his MBA degree in hand. I was sick of failing. I was also sick of pursuing careers for anyone other than myself. My years-old interaction with Professor Ryder came back to mind, and it was finally clear what I needed to do: my life had to be in food. That's right: finally, fatty was going to have his day in the sun!

There's a saying in French: *Le cordonnier, toujours le plus mal chaussée.* In other words, the shoemaker, always with the most unkempt shoes. It's a phenomenon pervasive to many industries, obviously. As it pertains to food, the chef, after possibly feeding hundreds of accolade-garnering meals to customers, comes home and shoves boxed macaroni and cheese in their mouth. That was never me. I may not have always respected my body, but man did I respect my palate.

I moved back to Montreal and decided to put my MBA knowledge (if not degree per se) to use for my new career in food. I started small: a catering company, operating out of my parents' garage. And yes, for the food nerds and rule followers out there, that *did* fly in the face of a number of laws around health, safety, and hygiene. But don't you fret—I had my mother reminding me of exactly that on a regular basis.

> "Somebody in the neighbourhood is going to tell on you and
> your business is going to be shut down!"
> "I *know*, Mom. So, if you would kindly lower both your voice
> and the garage door, we'll be closer to reducing that possibility."

I was keen to make a name for myself as a caterer and figured the best way to do that would be to come up with some signature dishes. I came out swinging, as the saying goes. In the years right after 2001, the country of Afghanistan was being mercilessly bombed in what most of us recognize as a fraudulent retaliation for 9/11. Who was doing any positive PR for Afghanistan in those days? No one! I decided that through my food, *I* was going to hold Afghanistan up (or Afghan food at the very least) in a positive light. Sure, these catering gigs for thirty people weren't exactly going to put me up for a Nobel Peace Prize, but I recognized an opportunity to do some good.

I started making "Afghan naan pizzas." No one had ever heard of them because I essentially created them: take the four-foot-long Afghan naan, brush the bottom with olive oil, top with a sun-dried tomato pesto, caramelized onions, and crumbled Bulgarian feta, then bake it until crisp, top with fresh basil and tarragon, and serve in small squares. It wasn't rocket science, but it was my little attempt to make a difference with the opportunities I had.

I also started offering cooking classes around Montreal and Eastern Ontario: at local grocery stores, cookbook shops, and even at one beautiful, converted abbey in Ontario. At first, my plan was to teach "Mediterranean cuisine." At any given moment, Mediterranean food could mean Spanish, Greek, French, Provençal, Moroccan, Turkish, Italian, and much more. So, this was really just my "teaching hack" to keep me from getting bored of teaching one thing over and over again. But as I got started, the students (middle-aged white women with European heritage, primarily, who could have probably taught me as much as I taught them!) would inevitably ask me where I was from. I would say, "South Asia. My parents are Pakistani, and our ancestors are Indian." And without fail, they would all say, "Well, we'd *love* to learn Indian and Pakistani cuisine!" Who was I to not give the people what they wanted?

I started making Indian- and Pakistani-influenced dishes for my catering events, as well. Not the on-the-nose butter chicken and saag paneer stuff, but dishes that would make a guest stop and think, *There are definitely some South Asian notes in this dish.* For example, I was putting my own spin on an Italian frittata by toasting cumin seeds, then sautéing them with leftover tandoori chicken and a small amount of finely grated ginger and adding a beaten-egg mixture full of fresh cilantro. Voilà, the tandoori chicken frittata was born! I would also serve a puff pastry stuffed with spicy, roasted eggplant purée (*baingan bharta*) and provolone, and a dinner menu would often include a spicy South Asian version of a French bouillabaisse.

It was a new level of creativity, and I was having a ton of fun with it. And, of course, true to my roots as the son of the Dawson College Samosa Man, I was making my own samosas. So *many* samosas. My fingernails would be stained with turmeric for days after rolling and stuffing a few hundred of them. Before possibly earning some nickname like "Ol' Yellow Fingers Hassan," I quickly added gloves to my catering inventory.

The catering and cooking classes were reconnecting me with my heritage. The irony was not lost on me: the enthusiasm of various white people was actually bringing me back to the food I ran from as a child. I didn't run from eating it, mind you, but the smell that embarrassed me in my youth was now one that I was standing directly in, serving with a smile, and teaching others how to create. I'm not certain if I was an honorary Pakistani just yet, but I was definitely paying tribute to my heritage. My parents, as proponents of trivial things like job security and higher education, were not particularly pleased, but something more important than that had happened. For the first time in what felt like forever, I was doing work that I loved.

Chapter 15

THE DAY I LEARNED WHAT PASSION IS

I LOVED EATING FOOD. I loved making food. Some might have suggested that I was even obsessed with it. But I didn't know if I was truly "passionate" about it. Like, everyone sounds like they're passionate about food when they are describing meals that they love!

Although it bears mentioning that I know two people who have independently said to me that they find eating two to three times a day to be such an inconvenience that they both wished they could take a pill, once every morning, to satisfy all their daily nutritional and caloric needs, thereby doing away with the "nuisance" of having to find food or buy food or, worst of all, eat food. I'm not joking. That there would be one such person alive is bewildering. But the fact that *I personally* know two of them, suggests there are many others out there. My God, that makes me uncomfortable. Now, it *could* be argued, as someone who complains about the sluggishness of human digestion and the "unfair space limitations" of his stomach, I might be on an equally unhealthy opposite end of that spectrum.

So, I'm a glutton. Is gluttony passion? How does one know that they are truly passionate about something? Well, I discovered the answer to that through a strange intersection of friendship, an island wedding nearly gone awry, and extreme exhaustion.

I met my buddy Dave at McGill University. Very soon after first meeting him, we all started to call him Triniboy Dave—which was odd, because now his nickname was longer than his actual name. Also, we had no other Daves in our group of friends. The nickname wasn't even necessary. Were we planning for the inevitable future meeting and enjoyable company of a second Dave? In the end, I think the Trini part had to do with the fact that his Trinidadian identity was so intricately woven—for better or worse—into so much of what he did.

"It's January, how come Dave isn't wearing socks?"
"Oh, he's from Trinidad."
"Why does Dave's fridge have seven different hot pepper sauces
    in it, and nothing else?"
"Oh, he's from Trinidad."
"Why did Dave wake up at three a.m. to listen to a cricket match?
    On the radio. In Australia."
"Oh, he's from Trinidad."

My favourite thing to witness was when someone asked Dave where he was from. It would always unravel in the following way. *Trinidad.* If no other question was asked, he was quite happy to have someone think he got off a boat from Trinidad a month ago. But you know people and their pesky curiosity. The more they asked, the closer he would get to the truth. *Canada.* Oh, but where? *I have family in Toronto. But I'm basically a Montrealer.* Where in Montreal? *Okay, well, technically, it's Halifax!* And then I always felt compelled to add, "He was born in Dartmouth, Nova Scotia!" and Dave would aggressively shush me. Apparently, everything that Dave was and loved was not celebrated in Dartmouth, Nova Scotia, in the seventies and eighties when he was growing up.

After McGill, Triniboy Dave left Montreal to pursue his master's degree in Ottawa. Although I was initially sad that he was leaving Montreal, I was happy to hear that he and his longtime girlfriend, Sonia (as we'll call her), were still going to try to work things out. It appeared that I would still get to see Triniboy Dave from time to time on certain weekends. The thing is, we started noticing that we were seeing a little "too much" of Dave on the weekends. Having drinks in someone's backyard—Triniboy Dave is here! Going to a late-night movie—Triniboy Dave is here! Kicking around a soccer ball at 10 a.m. in a random park—Triniboy Dave is here? At some point, as his friend, I had to ask about it: "Dave, you come back to Montreal to visit Sonia, but it doesn't seem like you're seeing much of Sonia. What's the deal here?" He gave it to me straight. "Bro, the truth is, I'm not passionate about Sonia."

"What the hell does that mean, 'you're not passionate about her'? You come back practically every weekend to visit her, you're racking up hundreds of dollars in monthly long-distance bills talking to her on the phone all week long, and even the one time I came to visit you in Ottawa, you were on the phone with her for almost the entire weekend!"

"Man, I love her. And I'm in love with her. But I'm not passionate about her."

"You lost me."

"Let me put it this way. When you see your girlfriend, after you haven't seen her for a week or so, do you want to just rip off her clothes and jump into bed?"

"Sure, sometimes even after even a day or two of not seeing her."

"Yeah. I don't have that feeling. At all."

To hammer home a point that I'm sure has already been made: one time, during the week, Dave even told his girlfriend that he had been hit in the penis with a baseball, and thus couldn't engage in any upcoming weekend "activities," just to get out of them. The issue that he didn't ever really play baseball didn't seem to come up.

So, that's one way of looking at passion: by its absence. But how do you know you have it? I came to a point in my life where my love for food was so strong that it became my favourite thing to read about, think about, and talk about. I had subscriptions to three different food magazines, and I watched hours and hours of shows on the Food Network (it helped that I was largely unemployed during that time, but that's beside the point)—and I'm talking about the *early* years of the Food Network, when there were maybe five hundred of us worldwide watching this thing. It was still years away from becoming the refuge of the armchair chef. I still remember a show that Bobby Flay used to do in a kitchen in an NYC loft apartment, with a live audience of about fifteen people in front of him, accompanied by a woman named Jacqui, who was apparently a Canadian comedian. It was like watching a chef open mic. I was watching him develop his personality, live on television. I've met a total of four people who remember that show.

One day, living out my catering dreams in Montreal, and most likely watching the Food Network, I got a phone call from a friend who I had gone to university with: Ahmer. He lived in NYC now and was marrying a lovely Colombian woman and explained that they planned to come back to Canada to get married, on a place called Toronto Island. He had heard from mutual friends about my catering ventures and he explained that they'd both love it if I could cater their special day. Did I know anything about the hall they were getting married in? No. Did I know anything about Toronto Island? No. In fact, when he mentioned where he was getting married, I remember thinking, *This poor guy thinks Toronto is an island. Oh well, I'll let him know when I get there.* Did I even know a thing about catering in the city of Toronto? Also, no. But I'll tell ya what I did know: I had a sordid, lengthy history of—if you'll excuse the food metaphor—biting off more than I could chew. So, this event felt very on-brand for me.

To use a comparison from the comedy world, if you're a comedian and a show producer asks you if you have twenty minutes of a material, basically every single comedian who has five minutes of tested material will say yes, and they will assume/pray that the other fifteen will come to them in the form of organic material onstage and banter with the audience. This often doesn't go well. In any case, I had this attitude already and I wasn't even in the comedy world yet. I was ahead of my own time, you could say. In the catering world people would ask me if I'd ever catered for 150 people and I'd say, "Obviously, man!" but what was actually obvious was that I had maybe fed a maximum of seventy-five people, perhaps one time. That said—and lies and exaggerations aside—this one was important. Ahmer was a friend. His fiancée trusted him to trust me. Their friends and guests were trusting me. I was going to do whatever it took to not let them down.

To that end, a month before the wedding, I drove the five hours from Montreal to Toronto to do some early reconnaissance work on local bulk food purchases, equipment rental, and travel to and from the wedding venue. I found out pretty quickly that *I* was the fool. Not only was there such a thing as Toronto Island, but it was a collection of several islands. But unlike the island of Montreal, which was accessed via your choice of various bridges, access to the Toronto Islands was instead limited to travel by boat. Bridges, you see, would have led to a lot of people coming onto the islands. And, as I eventually learned, if there was one thing that the assemblage of hippies, loners, and weirdos who made up the residents of the Toronto Islands did not like, it was people. To this day, it's still unclear to me how any of them make a living and if they are even connected via phone or internet to the rest of the world.

In any case, I organized an early meeting with the owner of the hall, at the hall. Upon meeting him, I said, "I couldn't help but notice that I had to get here by boat. Is there a way that I'll be able to bring all my food and equipment here in a van on the day of the event?" And his response was "I think so?" As a question. He responded to my question about how to come to the hall he owns on the island he lives on with a less clear question. To this day, if you google "Are there cars allowed on Toronto Island?" you will get this as a response:

> The Toronto island community is considered to be the largest urban car-free community in North America, although some service vehicles are permitted.

Was I going to be one of those "permitted vehicles"? Was my wedding catering a "service"? This idiot certainly wasn't going to tell me. He didn't even "answer" as much as he "mumbled" while he continued to rummage through the cupboards of the kitchen area to show me all the shelf space I would have access to on the day of the event.

To its credit, the kitchen was spacious. Not a plate or glass in sight, but there was certainly a lot of prep and counter space, plus two fridges, a flat-top oven, and a stove. And I knew enough about catering at the time to also ask about the oven—specifically about its strength and reliability. I was hoping he'd be more forthcoming with an answer here than he was about transportation, and he was, but it was almost less helpful. When I asked, "Does the oven work well?" he said—and I quote—"Yes, but I mean, like, don't use it *too* much, or anything." That was really a moment for me to pause and ask, "What the hell are you saying, sir?" But in my head, I thought, *This guy understands that I'm going to cater a wedding for 150 people. Obviously, he understands that catering involves cooking and that cooking involves using an oven.* In retrospect, I assumed too much.

In any case, I headed back to Montreal, and with an even greater sense of excitement I started planning the menu for this wedding. The couple had suggested that a Mediterranean menu might be nice, and I couldn't have agreed more. I also started booking the staff for the event—read: calling my friends in Toronto. My first call was to Triniboy Dave. As well as holding a master's degree in pharmacology *and* being a lawyer, Dave was also a great cook. Once Triniboy was enthusiastically on board, this started to feel more like a party than work. I recruited about five other friends—even my ex-girlfriend offered to come along, because apparently those wounds had healed, and she'd bring her best friend, too, and some other people who had some experience serving food. The Toronto Island Catering Posse was in place.

Two days before the wedding, I rented a van in Montreal and went by myself (Toronto Island Catering Posse had the limitation of living *in* Toronto) to a party rental place I did occasional business with, to pick up a hundred and eighty of everything: plates, smaller plates, bowls, water glasses, wineglasses, forks, spoons, plus napkins and tablecloths. It was a genuine nightmare visualizing how we were going to transport this to an island, and I tried not to think about it, because every time I did, my only thought was *You really didn't think this through.* Why didn't I just rent this stuff in Toronto, you might be wondering? Great question, and I have no answer for it.

The day before the wedding, I drove to Toronto and went to a variety of shops and food supply stores to pick up all the raw food that I needed. That night I parked in Dave's condo building, prayed to God that the van and its rented contents wouldn't get stolen, and we started prepping some of the food and shoving all the rest of it in his very basic Toronto condo-sized fridge.

It turned out it was a very complicated affair indeed to get everything onto the island. I'd learned that there was a small bridge that was "sometimes" open, on which you could "possibly" take a van across, but then you'd have to wind through a number of other islands to get to *this* island and, if you can believe it, it was easier to take nine small water taxis across at once, filled with "staff," food, equipment, and rented glasses, cutlery, and utensils. But note that "easier" did not in any way resemble "easy."

On the day of the wedding, we set out early in the morning, the whole bunch of us, to take the water taxis across the lake. A few of the taxis had to carry just one human being, surrounded by crates of food and kitchen supplies. We hit the island and unloaded all the crates and boxes into the kitchen and started preparing and cooking, even though it wasn't even 11 a.m. There was a lot to do, because, in retrospect, I went overboard (pun very much not intended, and thank God no one actually went overboard—I didn't have the managerial acumen to lose someone in Lake Ontario and still cater a successful event) in my proposed catering menu.

The challenge with hiring a crew that is predominantly your friends is that you can't effectively boss anyone around. My ex's best friend would get distracted constantly with conversations with wedding guests. One nice outfit on a guest and she disappeared to ask them where they'd bought it. Triniboy was taking what felt like superlong cigarette breaks, which I had no control over. And my friend Arsalaan was constantly flirting with the servers we had hired. Arsalaan, by the way, was a bank teller for a summer and his boss had to reprimand him once, saying, "Arsalaan, please don't skip to the vault." I knew this, and still hired him. So that was on me.

My specialty was always appetizers. That's what I did best, and it was also probably connected to how quickly I got bored. Appetizers were a way to shake up the palate, and even the energy of a party, if they were done right. So I had planned, in my overzealousness, to make eight appetizers and basically "release" a new one every twenty to thirty minutes over the first three hours. Guests were impressed, full, and really satisfied before the outdoor wedding ceremony began. My friends got married in front of a gorgeous sunset—a blazing blue-orange hue rippling across the lake. If there was a moment where

I could have appreciated Toronto Island it was then, but it was fleeting since I still had dinner to cook, and at the very back of my mind was the disbelief that we still had to eventually take so much crap back to the city on boats, and this, too, against the clock, before the boats stopped running.

The stars of the Mediterranean dinner menu were the following: a baharat chicken, which consisted of chicken thighs and a seven-spice mixture called baharat that I had marinated overnight in a garlic-yogurt marinade in Triniboy Dave's fridge; *imam bayildi*, which is a famed baked eggplant dish that translates into "the imam fainted"—the lore being that a certain imam came home one day, smelled this eggplant dish that his wife had cooked, and fainted. Realistically, it's more likely that he fainted from hypertension, or a minor cardiac episode brought on from all the oil clogging up his arteries from years of eating dishes like these. And then my tarator fish. Oh, that fish. The dish that turned out to be the bane of my existence for an evening. It was a thin sole that would, in theory (and in centuries of actual practise), take no time at all to cook, so it stood to reason that it should go in the oven last.

I baked the eggplant first and kept it warm, and then we baked the chicken. And then it was time for the fish to go in. It occupied all three shelves of the oven and it was the final component of our meal. And every time I opened the oven door, it was still not done. We waited another few minutes—the guests were all in the hall now, sitting, chatting, and waiting for a dinner that was already scheduled to be on the later side, to be eaten after a July sunset—opening the oven door to again discover that the fish was still mostly raw. Why? Why! It was a very simple thing, this recipe. This fish was to be seasoned with salt, baked on a high heat for less than ten minutes, and then destined to meet its mate: a delicious and tangy tarator dressing, made of tahini, lemon juice, garlic, parsley, cumin seeds, and chili flakes—and dammit, it was just that simple, but why wouldn't the fish hurry up and bake?!

And suddenly the words of that son of a bastard of a hall owner—a month prior—came back to me: "Like, don't use it too much or anything." It was now dawning on me what this meant: *You can bake several appetizers in this oven. You can then bake one hundred chicken thighs in this oven. And then you can bake stuffed eggplant in this oven to your heart's content. But, if after all that, you try to bake some soft, thin, tender, flaky sole fillets in this oven, you will be screwed.* And indeed, I think it was Triniboy Dave who pointed it out: we were screwed.

The oven, set to 450 degrees Fahrenheit, was now giving off a "warmth" you might get from a light breeze on a sunny October morning in Canada. I had planned the menu well, I had planned and bought the right amount of food, I had hired the right number of staff, I had finally *not* bitten off more than I could chew—and this goddamned oven was going to ruin everything!

The kitchen was tense and silent, and everyone looked at me. My serving staff was wondering when dinner was going to be ready (probably because they eventually wanted to go home), and my kitchen staff, composed of no one with actual restaurant experience, had already long surpassed the limits of their capacity to stand on their feet and were also concerned. Some were likely wondering why we couldn't just scrap the fish altogether. My vision for a well-rounded menu and my hatred for wasting food could never allow that to happen. No, this moment now called for honesty. Honesty that could buy us some time while we cooked the fish in pans or in chafing dishes. I'd have to let the guests know what was happening. I pulled Ahmer aside.

"Ahmer, I need to make an announcement to the guests," I said. "Of course, bro!" He was so wrapped up in the joy of his amazing day that he didn't even notice how tense I was. He brought me out into this hall that was just reverberating with overwhelmingly positive vibes, and I was sickened by the fact that I was about to change that energy.

"Everyone. Everyone! Can I introduce our chef to you—my friend, Ali Hassan!" The entire hall erupted in applause and cheers. "Oh God," I muttered, to myself (hopefully). It was too much. Just too much cheering. I started to feel knots form in my stomach. But my policy was to lead with honesty.

"Hi, everyone. I wished you hadn't clapped that much because you don't know what I'm about to tell you. There's a bit of an issue in the kitchen. I know, it's a poor craftsman who blames his tools, so please forgive me. Almost all of the food is ready, but there is a fish dish that isn't cooking because the oven has regressed to the wattage of an Easy-Bake Oven and it's just going to take some time—maybe thirty more minutes before we get dinner out." There was a pause. Everyone looked at each other . . . and then burst into cheers and applause again! What? Okay, that went bizarrely well. I walked back into the kitchen and exhaled. "They're drunk and we're going to be okay!"

The truth is, while alcohol and unbridled joy did play a role that day, the thing that really wound up saving my ass was that I was "an appetizer guy." These people were well-fed and content, and dinner at this point was just a bonus. In thirty minutes, the food was in chafing dishes and the guests were happily lining up to eat. I always said that if I enjoy my food, then I know the clients will enjoy it. That food really was a hit.

We started our cleaning and packing up, washing our pots and pans and putting the rented cutlery and dinnerware back into the crates they came in. Among the things Toronto Island did not invest in was lighting. And so we hurried dozens and dozens of crates and boxes to the dock area in pitch-darkness. The many boats and water taxis that exist all day long seem to disappear by the night. They've had enough by nighttime. And our drivers were really displeased with all the stuff that was going to go on their boats and how long it was clearly going to take to load and then unload it all on the other side. We left Toronto Island for the final time close to midnight, unloaded all our stuff on the mainland dock, and I went to get the van from Dave's apartment. Out of mercy, I let all my friends/staff go home and it was just Dave, Arsalaan, and me left to load everything back into my rental van. I couldn't imagine what my staff was feeling, because even I—a man who made his living as a caterer—was in physical pain. My back was on the verge of seizing up, and my knees were crying out for me to sit down for even a few minutes. My gluttony also meant I was very overweight, and that was making all things worse.

By the time it was all said and done we were back in Triniboy Dave's apartment at 2 a.m., collapsed on his couch and laughing about the insanity of the day. In a moment of silence, Dave remembered something. "Damn, I still have some lamb chops sitting in my fridge, marinating from two days ago. I was going to make those tonight but didn't realize we'd be back so late." He shrugged, but then added, "We *could* head to my rooftop and grill that lamb and have some wine, if you're up for it?"

I feel like *anybody* else in that moment would've said, "Are you insane? After fourteen hours of standing on our feet and prepping and cooking and lifting and loading and unloading multiple times, you want to go up and stand around some food again and cook something?" In fact, I think Arsalaan did say all of that. But I didn't hesitate. It sounded like the best way to indulge ourselves after the day we'd had. Dave got his lamb out, and I grabbed the wine. And a bottle of rum. We were celebrating, after all.

I realized that day I was truly passionate about food. Going up to the roof was a celebration of that fact. To paraphrase Triniboy's own anecdote from years prior, I gently but hungrily removed lamb chop's clothes that day—she loved me, and I loved her, and no one could ever tell me different. This is what passion felt like. And even if it took an expensive MBA and an even more expensive IT degree to get here, to *this moment*, I was finally and completely content with that. All my past failures—in education, in work, in my own path of self-discovery—had vanished and were replaced by a relatively unfamiliar feeling of pride and satisfaction.

On a final crazy note: Ahmer and his wife told me that their son was born nine months to the day of their wedding. They joked that "maybe it was something in the fish." But you know what, maybe when you operate from a place of passion, it fosters more passion in others. That's not such an unbelievable thought, after all.

Chapter 16

STAND AND DELIVER

WHEN YOU FIND A PASSION for food—or rather, *realize* that you have a passion for food—in your thirties, and combine that with an aggregate total of ten thousand hours of food television viewing experience, the following is bound to happen: you will start to imagine yourself with your own food television show. And since it's all in your imagination, you imagine that you're pretty awesome at it. Ostensibly, no one's overcooking the steak in their fantasies.

I started watching cooking shows as a curious preteen. Jacques Pépin and Julia Child were as interesting to me as cartoons might have been to any other child. By the time I was in my thirties, however, that curiosity had been replaced by frustration. I was yelling at the food shows the way fifty-year-old men interact with NFL football games: "What—you're not gonna squeeze some lime on that? Way to blow a great opportunity!" Or, "What the hell, Emeril, why does the audience keep swooning every time you say, 'Gaaaahhhlic'? You'd throw some chilies into that stew if you had any self-respect!" And, "Did you just make a pun about thyme and time? Come on, man, what is this, the seventies?! COACH, THROW ME IN THERE! I CAN SAVE THIS!" Now, it bears mentioning that some of those television chefs were truly masterful, but others, well, let's say they gave me the inspiration that I, too, could clearly host my own show. I sat on my couch, zero television experience or proven talent, *knowing* that I could do better than half of them. What a dummy.

In 2005, I had been living with my girlfriend in small-town Ontario, where she was working as a doctor. I was commuting back and forth to my hometown of Montreal for my steadily decreasing catering gigs. The key to catering, I had learned, is to be on people's radar. You may blow a client's mind with the most exciting Caribbean-inspired, Scotch bonnet–forward curried goat, but a year later when they host their annual party again, they've already had a dozen people tell them about another caterer they "just *have* to try." As a caterer, it became clear to me that being "on the radar" meant having to attend parties and events so that people could see me, and we could have some variation of the following together:

"Wait, do I know you?"

"It's possible."

"Are you a caterer?"

"Yup. Ali Hassan."

"I think you catered my sister's fortieth birthday party on the West Island a few years ago."

"I'm sure I did!"

"I still remember those lamb chops you made! Do you have a card?"

"Umm . . . let me see. You know what, I just might, in fact."

In *fact*, I had ten thousand, because you really got a deal per unit when you got them in bulk. But as I tried to work on my small-town relationship (with both the girlfriend and the town), I became less and less able to attend events in Montreal. And while I was getting increasingly creative with my food, my ingredients, and my presentation, I was living (read: slowly decaying) in a place that one local resident described to me as "a real meat 'n' potatoes town." I found myself suffering in a town that my girlfriend and I had both taken to calling "the place where creativity comes to die."

A truly amazing coincidence was that in this town of 2,500 people, there was actually a woman looking to sell her existing catering company. And here I was, a caterer, looking for some steady work. This should have been incredible news. She was willing to sell all her equipment and her entire client list. In Year 1, I would make enough to pay that all off, and by Year 2 the business would be all profit. I was intrigued until we chatted on the phone, and she told me, "We pretty much *own* the funeral market in this area." That was her sales pitch. It didn't land the way she thought it would. Had I been the type of man who was motivated by money, perhaps this might have been an appealing offer. But I was always motivated by the work. And in this case, no amount of funeral catering was going to excite me.

Small-town life and my small-town relationship came to an end by Christmas 2005, and I kicked off my 2006 motivated in a way that I had never been before. Leaving that town, a place that more people died in than moved to, was the closest I've ever felt to being released from prison (every recess at Sunday school was a close second). I was thrown back into gen pop ("general population," in case you haven't done time or spent hours watching prison shows), and I couldn't wait to start my life *for real.* I had a goal, nay, a singular unwavering focus: to become the host of my own television cooking show.

I wasted zero time in working toward it. I read about food, I watched food television, and I signed up for local food conferences, symposiums, and seminars. There was nothing I didn't want to know about food. *Food security?* Bring it on, let's feel safe together. *Food waste.* I hate it, let's talk about it. *The future of food?* I don't know what it is, but let's grow old together.

At one such food conference, I spotted a lovely woman named Elizabeth Baird, standing by herself and perusing a snack table. I recognized Elizabeth from television. She was the head of *Canadian Living* magazine and part of a trio of women from the magazine who hosted their own television cooking show. I thought, *Why don't I just go ask her what she thinks about how someone might get their own food show on television, short of becoming an editor for a top Canadian lifestyle magazine?* She was welcoming and lovely and even directly answered my question: "Spend as much time in front of the camera as you can." I thanked her profusely for her time and that answer. As she walked away, I realized that I really needed to work on my follow-up-question game. Questions like "What does that even mean?" or "How do I do that?" would have been useful. It's not like there are cameras stationed at every corner of the city waiting for people to get in front of them! But she had reimmersed herself into a crowd of people and I was left alone to consider her advice. *How could I put that suggestion into practise?*

I reflected on this for a few days, and the answer came to me: I would reach out to my people. I contacted the local South Asian community television program to see if they would have me on to do a food segment. They bit (pun intended), and we filmed a fun segment of me walking along Jean-Talon Street in Montreal, dipping in and out of South Asian grocers and explaining all the foods I picked up and why. I enjoyed the whole day, and the host and I had a great rapport. Once it was all edited and packaged, he even emailed me to say it looked great, and "my boss said he'd love to have you back!"

Yes! Nothing like instant success. Waiting around and paying your dues is for suckers! I messaged him back and said, "Sure, how's next week?" There was probably an awkward moment on his end when he read that, because the poor guy had to send me a long email explaining how community programming worked. The South Asian community was sizable in Montreal and only given sixty minutes a week on this network. Many different groups, subgroups, fringe communities, event organizers, and various talented Brown folk were vying for a spot on the show. He ended his email with "How about I hit you up again in about six months?"

I went back to the proverbial drawing board. Camera time, camera time, where *are* you! I had another idea. One that would prove to be pretty fundamental to the rest of my life: What if I performed on open-mic comedy shows? No, it wasn't in front of a camera, but there were similarities. There was a stage, an audience—I could treat them like a studio audience, all the while building my own confidence, my persona, and telling jokes about food.

It made sense. I'd been hosting weddings for the last decade. When close friends were getting married and the couple needed a host, they often thought of me. I'm certain it had everything to do with my talents and nothing to do with saving money (let me have my dreams). The point is, I was hosting *South Asian* weddings—if you've been, you know they aren't a small affair. Unless it's someone's third wedding, 350 to 500 guests are the norm. I had been getting in front of large crowds and entertaining them.

The challenge was that my performances heretofore were catered specifically to the wedding, the happy couple, and their guests. My bit about Nirav being an accountant, and his bride, Anu, being a urologist, and their future kids being good at counting penises probably wasn't going to fly at open-mic night in downtown Montreal on a Monday. And if I was being honest, I was getting pretty tired of those weddings. Between the hosting, attending, and working at weddings as a chef, I was averaging at least a dozen South Asian weddings a year. It was time to get on a real stage (i.e., not a wedding hall) in front of real audiences (i.e., paying audiences) and tell *real* jokes. There was one small hitch: I didn't exactly know what real jokes were.

It was time to write some material. While I can't recall exactly what those first jokes were, I do remember my friend Q inviting me to his basement music studio to record them. It wasn't about the recording, it was about practising using a mic. He even added laugh tracks to help me gain a feel for it. He recorded them all, and one day I'll have the courage to revisit and experience whatever collection of unoriginal poop and dick jokes I thought might be funny onstage. Hey, it's a journey.

Like a lot of new performers, my first time onstage, my five-minute set took me three and a half minutes to deliver live. Even though I had entertained hundreds of people in my community for years, this was completely different. It was beyond thrilling to be in this brick-lined room, with the words THE COMEDYWORKS behind me, making a room of forty *paying* strangers (and Q and Zach Moos, who were there for the support) laugh. I barrelled through my first set, and as I walked off stage my knees almost buckled, as if to say, "What the hell did you just do, man?"

That exhilaration I felt was the beginning of a brand-new career. I wanted to do that again. I wanted to feel that thrill again. I did it a few more times, and the sound guy and the waitress—Eman, who became one of my closest friends—both told me that I should come back. They didn't pump my tires too much, but told me that I was good. Eman added, "I hope you continue with it." Someone who sees comedy every day as part of their job, telling me I should keep at it, was all the motivation I needed. To this day, I can't understand how comedians bomb the first several times onstage and keep coming back. I respect it enormously, but I can't understand it. A flop that first night would have discouraged me forever.

The ComedyWorks was also where I met Jimbo. He was the owner of the club and the bar located directly underneath it. Many of my first open-mic sets ended with me singing Frank Sinatra on karaoke, arm in arm with Jimbo. Quite soon after, Jimbo got rid of the karaoke machine (unrelated to my singing), and I was forced to focus on the quality of my material.

In the United States, between the 1920s and 1960s, there was an area in upstate New York called the Catskill Mountains that came to be known as "the Borscht Belt." It was a popular place for Jewish families from New York City to vacation, and it stood to reason that it would also become a very popular and profitable place for Jewish comedians to practise their craft. The comedy was, as was the style in those days, memorized stock jokes, sometimes altered slightly to be more entertaining for Jewish audiences. Jokes like "I just got back from a pleasure trip. I took my mother-in-law to the airport." And this would be told by someone who might not even have a mother-in-law. It was all schtick, and it needn't even be grounded in reality. In fact, it was inconceivable to get onstage and just talk about your actual life (many would thank Lenny Bruce and Mort Sahl for ushering in that format). So, the comedians all wound up having the same jokes. So much so that you'd often hear an audience member yell out from the crowd, "Heard it yesterday!"

In retrospect, at the start of my comedy career I probably should have received a few "heard it yesterdays" myself. It's not that I was recycling jokes, but I certainly wasn't being original or authentic. I was actually being a bit of a fraud. I didn't know what my voice was supposed to sound like, and to complicate matters—even though it was 2006—9/11 was still on people's minds. The security policies that were put in place because of the attacks were very fresh. I knew that firsthand because every time I was at an airport, something new and more thorough had been put in place.

Right after 9/11, at the airline ticketing counter, "We have to ask you a few more questions" became "We just need to make a call to transportation security—wait here." A year later, at the customs counter, "Go right ahead, we know you're not a dangerous Ali Hassan" became "Hey, we know you're not dangerous, but if you could just accompany us to secondary screening for a few minutes, that would be great." And by 2006, it was quite simply "Listen, man—there's a massive *X* that comes up when I scan your passport, so you're sitting in this windowless room and probably missing your flight because that's the way it is now."

All that led me to the conclusion that people in comedy clubs probably didn't want to hear from a Muslim Pakistani at that point in time. And so, my stage persona went through some rapid development.

STAGE 1: I flirted momentarily with a "Hi, everyone, I'm Ali, but it's actually short for Alejandro!" type of thing, with the possibility of doing my entire act as a Mexican character. But then thought better of it. The term "cultural appropriation" may not yet have been in common parlance, but it still felt gross. And also, how was being a Mexican going to help build my persona for the food television world? Focus, Ali. Focus!

STAGE 2: I was Ali Hassan, "Indo-Canadian comedian." I mean, it was *kind of* true? It's not completely untrue. It's only sort of not true. FINE, it was a lie. But it was a white lie. I looked at it like this: my parents were both born in India—my mother for real, and my dad because there wouldn't be a Pakistan for another eight years after his birth. I was *basically* Indian. "Folks, you know my people. We're harmless! We're the guys at call centres!" This lasted for a few months, but at the end of the day, the inconsistency of my last few years was just too blatant: How could I be doing positive PR for Afghanistan with Afghan bread at catered events, and then not do the same for Pakistan with my own voice onstage?!

STAGE 3: Every other comedian in those days seemed to have a "I'm one-half this, one-half that" joke. Like, "Hey, I'm half Cuban, half Irish. So I want to join the revolution, but I can't leave the bar!" While I may have judged some of these harshly at the time, I wound up coming up with one of my own. "Hey, I'm Ali. I'm half Pakistani and half . . . scared to admit that I'm Pakistani." It was my way out of Indian and into Pakistani, and it was only meant to be for a short time. It was a transitionary bridge, if you will.

STAGE 4: Finally, I came out of this phase of pretending to be something I wasn't, and I went to the well that many comedians start in: you joke about what you know. And as I've suggested, I knew about "The Room." And that was my first original joke: a three-minute bit about the secondary screening room at the airport that finally made me feel a little more like myself onstage.

The beauty of comedy was that it was also a place where everyone could belong. From awkward, introverted weirdos to handsome, assertive jocks to everyone in between—all were welcome. All people rendered equal by the stage and the audience. Comedy was the great equalizer. In the food world I would often watch a television show and wonder, "How did this goofball get on TV?" whereas comedy all made sense to me. If the audience thought you were original and funny, you brought the house down regularly, and you were a tough act to follow, you moved up in the comedy world.

I remember, alongside a number of my peers, watching a young comedian learn this the hard way. Her name was L.A., she was an attractive young woman, and a club owner felt she belonged onstage on the weekends. Based on what? Well, based on that aforementioned attractiveness. The regular open-mic comedians were outraged. "The weekends? The highly coveted, precious weekend work that was our reward for doing well during the week, over and over again?" L.A. had a good five minutes on a Monday and was promoted posthaste to the role of weekend host?

I mention her name because I remember thinking: *L.A.? She named herself Los Angeles? I mean, I've heard of fake it 'til you make it, but that's a little presumptive.* (I realize now she was probably a Laurie-Ann or something.) Regardless, all of us young, jilted comedians watched L.A. host a professional comedy club show on a Friday night. She opened with that good five minutes from her open-mic performance, and kind of stalled after that. By the time she brought up the opening comedian to stage (ten minutes in), she had already run out of material. She had nothing with which to bring up the middling comedian (I'm not being insulting, that's just want they're called in the lineup). There were some attempts at crowd work, but they didn't lead anywhere funny. Finally, it was time to bring up the headlining comedy—the point where the host is entrusted with making sure a crowd is jazzed and excited and truly warmed up—and she had nothing new or funny to say. She was humiliated, and through no fault of her own, L.A.'s comedy career came to a halt that night. Her weekend of work started and ended with a Friday night. And we all learned that skipping steps in stand-up comedy helped no one. Comedy was, and to me remains, the great equalizer.

While I may have started comedy as a means to an end, it took no time at all for me to realize that I now had two passions. Yes, this may seem greedy, but *all* of my twenties were spent professionally rudderless and joyless. The high from the audience's laughter, the challenge of writing good material, the new community of beautiful misfits that I had connected with—I couldn't have left it behind if I'd wanted to.

Chapter 17

THE ROOM

WHILE I WAS NOW SPENDING a fair amount of time in comedy clubs—the great equalizer—I also happened to be spending time in a place of great division.

They say that when you start in stand-up comedy, you typically joke about what you know. Post-9/11, there were two things I knew very well: what people thought of people with my background, and what the inside of an airport secondary screening room looked like.

My look and my name reinforced my Muslim identity at airports, in particular, in the years that followed 2001. Every time I travelled—to the room. Going to Los Angeles? You'll get there eventually, sir, but first, *the room*. Headed to Houston? Terrific! But we'd like to ask you a few questions. *In the room*. Attending a wedding in Tobago? That's wonderful, señor. But now that you're halfway there, in Miami, we'll need to ask you some questions. *In the room*, por favor. And yes, you'll need to turn off your phone and your three friends can wait inside the airport and just wonder if you're alive or not for the next five hours.

That time, I missed my connecting flight to Trinidad (and so did my loyal friends) because of how long it takes for absolutely *nothing* to happen. That one irritated me quite a bit because Miami was just a stop to change planes. But being on American soil meant being subjected to US Customs and Immigration. "But I'm not staying here! I'm not even leaving the airport. If you let me get on my connecting flight, in just a few hours I'll be Trinidad and Tobago's problem!" All pleas fell on deaf ears.

The drama wasn't just reserved for transnational flights. Once, on Christmas Day, I even missed a flight from Montreal to Halifax. The plane took off as I was stuck waiting for the ticket agent, who was on hold for almost an hour with transportation security.

There have also been numerous car searches at the border, driving from Montreal to Boston or New York City. For many of those trips I was travelling with my buddy Qurram. *Qurram Hussain.* Even we had to admit that the optics weren't great on a Hassan and a Hussain travelling together in the early 2000s.

It got to a point where I would hand my passport to a customs officer and a large *X* came on the screen. I would already be moving in the direction of the room. I wasn't scared, really. But I was unhappy—with the state of affairs, with the reaction that my background, look, and name received. But you can only control what you can control. And with that in mind, I started considering a name change.

Al Hassan came to mind first. That would be the easiest to get used to.

Allan Hassan was less vague and at least half non-Muslim.

Allan Hanson was definitely considered. The musical group Hanson, those three blond teen brothers, was very big then. Maybe I was thinking I could ride that blond, white wave for a while.

And again, like when I first considered stage personas for comedy, I thought about Alejandro. I always thought about that name. I'm not kidding about that, either. I love the Spanish language and culture, and I was considering all my options.

My friend Aslam changed all that. I told him about the various steps and procedures I had been researching for a formal name change, and he told me, "Ali, the only thing worse than being an Ali Hassan is being someone formerly known as an Ali Hassan." His reasoning was that any security agency will know who you are now *and* will know who you used to be. So, they're just going to see a name change and wonder, "What's this guy hiding?" My enthusiasm for an identity change was officially squashed by that bit of wisdom.

I'm fully in support of tighter travel security, and it should surprise no one that I also want the airport and the "friendly skies" to be safe. But the fact that (even twenty years later), airport security couldn't just scan my passport and say, "Oh yeah, this guy, he's cool—we've background-checked him seventy-five times over the last decade," really worries me about the system. I've fantasized many times about having some wise-looking hooded companion standing ahead of me, waving his hand, and saying, "This isn't the Muslim you're looking for." Being innocent of any actual wrongdoing didn't matter, so maybe a Jedi mind trick couldn't hurt?

At the end of the day, I get it: "Ali Hassan"—shit name. There might be Ali Hassans who have done some awful things. But what truly puzzles me is this: Don't I—Ali Feryar Hassan—have some unique identifiers about me? Is there another Ali Hassan with that obscure middle name, who was born in New Brunswick, raised in Montreal, knows English, French, Urdu, and Punjabi, went to McGill University, is a comedian, has a birthmark below his left butt cheek, and loves to sing Bruce Springsteen's "Thunder Road" at karaoke nights? *Is there?* Because if there is, that person is my actual soul mate and I need to meet him *now*!

In the years after 9/11, my "luckiness" with random searches was getting downright obscene. But rather than dreading them, or letting them bother me, I tried to adopt a different attitude: the search is great for all of us! The employees at the airport now feel confident that I'm not a threat. And, as a bonus, all my fellow travellers can watch me get searched and now know they have nothing to worry about when they travel with Ali Hassan. "Ma'am, that suspicious look on the plane isn't necessary. Remember when I was getting patted down right beside the boarding gate as you guys watched along? Yeah, they didn't find anything! So, I'm cool. And look, I just ordered a beer. Would a terrorist order a beer? I'm just like you!"

These are the mind games that many Muslims or "Muslim-presenting" people have had to play. Because there is a real "Never let them see you sweat" vibe for a Brown Muslim who is travelling. You certainly can't let people see you angry. You don't have that privilege. That's kind of what they're waiting for.

At security, I decided that my arms would be up and my bag would be unzipped well before I was even asked. If they said, "We're not searching you, sir," that would be a pleasant surprise. And if they were searching, I was ready and happy to cooperate. Once, when I got that question I had heard dozens of times before—"Sir, have you ever been randomly searched before?"—I was in such a self-imposed good mood that I literally laughed out loud. "Man," I said to the security personnel, "I've been searched so many times, I think we can officially remove the word 'randomly' from it."

His response was curt and serious: "Have you ever been randomly searched by ME before?" I was reminded of two things in that moment. (1) Security needs to hear a very specific answer before they can move on to a particular task. I was in a flow chart! Don't bust the flow chart. (2) A positive attitude might help me personally, but customs and the border is not the place to joke around. Whether you're Brown or any other colour, it's ill-advised.

And by the way, it wasn't just me—the human being—having issues at the border. Products that I was ordering online—sweet, innocent products that had never harmed a soul (not fact-checked)—were also having issues. Worse issues, arguably.

One particular January, as I was searching for ways to be the "new me" and looking at pictures of cats with inspirational quotes above their heads (a favourite was "Way down deep, we're all motivated by the same urges, but cats have the courage to live by them"), I came across some solid advice from an American comedian, Rajiv Satyal. Rajiv had posted a blog about "HUSTLE" and he had referenced a type of resolution-making made somewhat famous by Jerry Seinfeld.

Basically, Jerry made an X on a calendar every day in which he achieved his goal: writing jokes. Eventually, wouldn't ya know it, Jerry had all these X's in a row on a calendar and he didn't want to "break that chain." One thing leads to another and he's one of the top-grossing comedians in the world. I'm skipping some steps here, but you get the idea. It was a calendar that encouraged consistency, something I desperately lacked. So, based on Jerry's success with this "Don't Break the Chain" method, and Rajiv's advice to buy a calendar that shows you the entire year in front of your face, I ordered a calendar: the key to my future success. Rajiv's recommendation was to buy it from a place called BusyBuildingThings.com (that'll be relevant in a moment).

After a week of waiting, I decided to go and track my package online. I found this notice when I entered the tracking number: *Five days ago, your package left Burbank, California, heading to Customs in LA.* Great! *The package remained in Customs for "Further Inspection."* Oooh—I don't like the sound of that. Two days later I checked back in, and the packaged had "arrived at its destination": Burbank, California. That's right, back from whence it came. This was particularly bad news because it was already late January at that point. I had procrastinated on buying the calendar, waiting until the new year was underway, and now customs was breaking a chain I hadn't even started yet!

I called USPS directly and they had no info for me. USPS transferred me to the international department, who "may have more info." They did not. But they did give me a number for US Customs. They would certainly have the info I needed, I was told.

It turned out that I couldn't even call their 1-800 number from Canada! You know that "This video has not been made available in your country" message you get sometimes when you're trying to watch a *Saturday Night Live* clip, for example, and you haven't downloaded an illegal VPN on your computer to circumvent that, like I one hundred percent haven't? I got that message, but with a phone number.

I was just about to call their direct number, and incur the associated long-distance charges, when it occurred to me: "Ali Hassan" is already a red flag at US Customs, so when he orders a package from a company called BUSY BUILDING THINGS, isn't that a deafening red siren? Never mind that the thing I ordered is just a glorified piece of paper—these guys will be damned before they help some Canadian Muslim achieve his annual "goals"! *You're busy, are ya fella? You're building "things," huh? Well, not on our goddamned watch you ain't!* (For best effect, you can read all that in the accent of a sheriff of a Southern American town, population 750.)

Needless to say, my productivity that year was nothing to write home about. And, of course, I am in no way maligning Rajiv, or Busy Building Things, or even Jerry Seinfeld. It's simply a case of Ali Hassan getting in the way of Ali Hassan, again. Just think of the top-grossing sitcom I could have had.

At one point, I had a bit of an epiphany. There was this new immigration policy that came in effect after 9/11 called biometrics that involved photographing and fingerprinting visitors to the US. I had even seen it happen right beside me in a customs lineup. Travellers being blindsided by a request to "put your fingers here, please" and having their prints and photos taken before they even knew what was really happening. It never happened to me personally; I was never even asked. They always seemed to be in far too much of a rush to get me seated in the room. VIP service, I guess.

Many of my Muslim friends were furious about this biometrics policy. I remember a friend, who is a lawyer, passionately yelling about how it was an infringement on human rights and a violation of privacy—and sometimes when a lawyer you know and trust is yelling stuff, you just feel inclined to agree with them. But then I gave it some actual thought. What the hell was *I* doing that was so *private* anyway? Oh, the government might find out that I was getting a hot dog at the Wiener's Circle at 2 a.m.? Or that I spent my entire Sunday from noon until 11 p.m. eating five thousand calories of snacks and watching NFL football at Duffy's Tavern? Who cares!

I realized I literally had nothing to hide. If there was a sting operation on me, the only thing that would come out of it would be some lowly FBI employee in a van telling their commanding officer, "Sir, we've been tailing this dude for a week—he seems to just want to kill himself, one corn dog at a time." Yes, my eating habits needed an overhaul, but that's just who I was then. None of what I was doing was illegal or even suspicious.

My lawyer friend wasn't in those rooms with me. He wasn't missing flights and getting pulled out of a boarding line to get patted down in front of fellow passengers. He hadn't even travelled to the US in years! If me getting fingerprinted meant that I could get to and from my destinations in the US without any hassle or delay, I was all for it.

It turns out, however, they don't do fingerprinting "by request." Customs officers don't like being treated like wedding DJs. "Bro, do my fingerprints and both my eyeballs!"—this wasn't going to work. So, I adopted the closest thing I could to having my privacy "invaded": I happily and confidently offered up *all* my information without a concern in the world. You want to know where I was on a particular night? I'll tell ya—I was eating three hot dogs, curly fries with gravy, and a strawberry milkshake. I normally wouldn't share all that with a stranger since it's kind of a disgusting and regrettable choice, but I want you to know everything about me!

When US Customs asked the standard question: "And what do you do in Canada?" I'd answer that I was a stand-up comedian. At a different time, I might have thought, *Don't tell them you're a comedian or they may think you're coming into the country to take stage time and money away from Americans!* So I started responding, "I'm a stand-up comedian. I'm going to perform at this particular club." And then I doubled down: "And I am going to take no money for it, because I am not allowed to make money in the United States." Confident honesty, and as a bonus, it also felt like the most nonthreatening thing I could say to a border guard. Stand-up comedian equalled fun-loving and harmless, and might even dilute the perceived "messiness" of my name. It was ingenious.

But it was also a strategy that backfired pretty quickly.

My wife has certainly had to suffer the consequences of travelling with Ali Hassan. But it's even more complicated. My sons and I have one last name, my daughters have their biological dad's last name, and my wife uses her maiden name. At a border, that is one car, six people, three different last names. And when you have *children* in a car with different last names, this *clearly* looks like an abduction situation—as far as my wife is concerned.

And she is already worried about the border. To make matters worse, any time we travel she has to get a letter from her ex-husband saying that he "allows" his biological children to travel outside of Canada. It's an unfortunate condition of their divorce. Especially unfortunate because the letter always looks like it's been written by a child. That's because, in a manner of speaking, it has been—a man-child. So, the night before we leave on a trip, as if the packing isn't stressful enough, my wife is also busy trying to print a letter that has spelling mistakes and nonsensical grammatical errors. Essentially, she starts visualizing an Amber Alert with our names on it and imagining a life of imprisonment for all of us. It's quite at odds with Ol' Honest Al.

On one road trip to New York, with her stress level in the car reaching its standard zenith a full fifteen minutes from the border, my wife was already in crisis mode. "Okay, everyone be quiet now!" Really? Fifteen minutes of quiet practise? Apparently, that time was for her to arrange and rearrange our passports by age several times, and to go over all the things she would and couldn't say when grilled mercilessly about who is in our car and why. I, of course, couldn't have been bothered with any of that. I had my own baggage to worry about. Not actual baggage, of course. We weren't smuggling Canadian fruit and cheap insulin across the border in our suitcases. I mean my years of pent-up, border-related emotional baggage. But, as was my policy, I would just go with honesty, because it allowed me to remain completely calm. *I've done nothing wrong and I'm telling the absolute truth.* On this particular trip, as we pulled up to the customs booth, I was successfully ignoring my wife's questions of "Does it look like I'm sweating? I feel like I'm sweating. Is the AC on max?" The interaction then went like this:

"Hello. Where are you going today?"

"Hi. We're headed to New York City."

"Passports, please."

(*Passports are handed over by me, as my wife's breathing becomes noticeably laboured.*)

"Who do we have in the car?"

"My wife, my two daughters, and my two sons."

"Mmm-hmm. And what are you going to New York City for?"

"I'm actually doing a set at a comedy festival. And I thought I'd bring my family along for a little trip."

"You're getting paid for that?"

"No, sir. I used to have a work visa many years ago, but without one now I just do the set for free. Just being part of the festival is something that's good for my promo and my brand."

(*This is the point where I can actually hear my wife's thoughts.* He's sharing too much. Why is he sharing so much?)

"So you're a stand-up comedian?"

"Yes."

"All right, let's hear a joke."

"Umm, yeah, a joke. I mean—to be honest, most of my jokes are
about my kids. And they're sitting right here, so it's gonna be
a little awkward, ha ha ha."
*(At this point, the border guard actually became that emoji with the
horizontal lines for eyes and a mouth.)*
"All right. Good luck with it."

He handed the passports back to me and we were on our way. My wife
immediately let out a massive sigh of relief and bewilderment. "Oh my God, I
can't believe he didn't even ask for the letter!"

All I could say was "The letter? Screw the letter! I can't believe I bombed
at the border again!"

And this has happened many times since. Somehow, that request from a
border guard always catches me off guard. Tell you a joke? Aren't we supposed
to talk about illegal firearms that I don't have, or the possibility of me having
luggage that I didn't pack myself? I thought I was supposed to be humourless
at the border. YOU trained me to never make jokes at the border! Now you're
requesting one? Do you have any idea how hard it is to go from *van dad*—
"Why are all those crumbs in your seat? Why didn't you go to the bathroom
before we left? What's that smell?"—to performing for an audience of one
border guard?

I've bombed at the border—that is to say, failed comedically—more times
than I like to recall. So many times, in fact, that one of the titles I proposed
for this book was *Bombing at the Border: The Ali Hassan Story*. But after some
thought, we all felt that it sounded way more aggressive than this book needed to.

I don't think any customs officer would say they are in the business of
providing "customer service," so I don't really know what to call what we get
from them. But honestly, my treatment in their hands has always been pretty
darn good. There was one exception, from way before 9/11.

My buddy Jasie and I were going skiing in Vermont, and we stopped at
the world's smallest car border crossing. No one was in the booth—the single
booth. We waited for a minute and figured they do things a little differently
at the world's smallest border. So, we got out of the car, stretched, and slowly

walked toward what can only be described as a hut. Suddenly a small, older customs officer came charging out of it, screaming bloody murder at us.

"Get back in that car immediately! Do you know it's a punishable offence to exit your car at an international border?" We jogged back to the car in a panic and stayed silent. "Well, *do* you?!" she repeated. Oh sorry, we thought that was a rhetorical question. "Passports!" she barked, now in her booth. We handed them over through the car window. She looked at my friend and said, "What's your name?" "Jasie," he replied. "Jasie what? We don't operate with just first names at a border!" There was no right answer with this officer.

After a few more minutes of similar scolding and border-crossing etiquette lessons, she let us go. It felt like that woman didn't like young Brown men, long before it was trendy. She was a pioneer, you might say. But here's what I believe the problem was (aside from us accidentally breaking the rule about not getting out of the car): I wasn't a stand-up comedian yet! I certainly wasn't going to tell her any jokes, but the truth, as odd as it seems, is that comedy affords me an increasingly better treatment at the border. (I'm reaching for some wood to knock on right now.)

Comedy has also shown me something about people we might otherwise write off as cruel or mean, without knowing them: their humanity.

I was flying from the Toronto Island airport to Boston once, and when you do that, you have to clear customs on the US side of your trip. Yeah, that's probably an expensive and embarrassing trip back if American customs doesn't accept you, and I have to admit, that's exactly what I was thinking about while I was sitting in secondary screening in the Boston airport.

I was asked, as was typically the case, to wait while some unanswered questions about me got answered. I was in full "Honest Al" mode that day, and had explained that I was a stand-up comedian when asked what it was that I did for a living. Apparently, word about that had spread among a number of officers on shift that day, and I literally had officers coming up to me and asking what it was like to be a comedian, who my favourite comedians were, and where I had performed. In the past I might have wondered, *Is this a trap?* but I quickly realized that it was simply human interest.

One customs officer said, "I got a joke for ya, tell me if you think this is funny"—and before I entered the very awkward possibility of telling a customs officer that their joke wasn't funny, a few of his colleagues jumped in and said, "Oh, don't listen to him, *we* don't even find him funny around here!" It was the closest thing a civilian could get to attending a border party. Truly. Finally, an officer came up to me and asked what type of comedy I did. I told him a joke that I had been "working on," thereby reducing his expectations.

It was a joke about the concept of "fine dining" and how overused and ridiculous that term had become. You go to an Indian buffet and the sign outside says FINE DINING. Interesting—so that spit shield covering the salad bar, is that part of the fine dining experience? You go to a Korean restaurant and the sign outside says FINE DINING. AND KARAOKE! Oh, okay. So that couple belting out Bon Jovi at table 7, have they had their fine dining experience yet, or is it after they sing "Livin' on a Prayer" out of sync?

He nodded his head and smiled, but didn't laugh. But then he did something that was better than anything else I could have ever hoped for. He gave me a joke.

"Yeah, that's funny," he said. "That's like here in Boston, it's really common for restaurants to call themselves 'World Famous.' Like *Pete's 'World-Famous' Hot Dogs*. Hey, Pete, you got a fifteen-square-foot establishment where your bathroom doubles for a mop closet. I'm pretty sure they're not talking about you in Istanbul or wherever right now. Anyway, you can use that if you want."

Something about my situation—sitting tight in a secondary screening room and having a customs officer with a Boston accent tell me that joke— made me laugh out loud. The whole thing, his joke included, was absolutely hilarious. And he ended with the words I had heard many times, "Hey, I'm sorry about this, by the way. We'll try to have you out of here as soon as possible." And for the first time, I felt like someone really meant it. I was out in fifteen minutes after that, and they all wished me well.

I tried for a year to make his joke work onstage, but I was never quite able to deliver it the way he had to me that day. But it didn't matter. The real gift wasn't the joke, it was the reminder of the power of comedy. My job as a stand-up comedian helped me, so very ironically, break down borders at the border. Customs in general, and the Room in particularly, might have elements that are designed to divide people, but I had this bizarre gift in my hands that allowed me to seek out the comedy there, and also bring it out onstage and in my writing. It was the craziest thing—my identity as a comedian was instrumental in helping me deal with my identity as a Muslim, which was often viewed as troublesome. That was the case in life, but it all started in the Room.

Chapter 18

THE HUMMUS FILES

ONE FINE DAY, a few months into my comedy career, I got a call from a guy named Amir Rizk. (This is back in the day when your phone rang and then you answered it.) Amir introduced himself as a host of a show on the McGill campus radio CKUT, a producer of a few other shows on the station, and a "lightning physicist."

I didn't know Amir—I guess you could say we didn't "travel in similar circles." But he had heard of me. And why not? What *wasn't* there to hear about? "Hey, there's this terrible local businessman, with a culinary profession from which he can't figure out how to make money, who has now added a second profession to his résumé, from which he somehow makes even *less* money" (chicken wings and drink tickets notwithstanding). I guess people were talking. Whatever the word on the street was, Amir was calling to invite me to be a guest on his show, and I figured all press is good press. If an interview on a campus radio station could put me in touch with even one person who was willing to pay me $12 a head for a catering event (dare to dream), it might be worth it.

The interview was about twenty minutes long: a semi-deep dive into my life featuring questions like "How does an IT consultant become a caterer and a stand-up comedian?" and "What do you like more: food or comedy?" It went fine. Truly, I might even have described it as borderline uneventful. Then, as Amir was wrapping up his cables and wires, an idea occurred to him.

"You know what, I think I have a proposition for you," he said. Fully expecting an Amway pitch, I reluctantly asked for more info. "I help to produce a show on CKUT called *Caravan*. Have you heard it?" I hadn't. "Well, it's an hour-long show where the host reads letters and emails that she receives from people around the world, who are stuck in war zones."

I waited a beat, and then said what I imagined was expected of me: "Okay, great! I'll keep my ears open for that one. Sounds exciting." But I'd misunderstood.

"No, no," he said. "Here's what I'm proposing. It's a very heavy show, emotionally. You are clearly a fun-loving, lighthearted guy with a good energy, and you have a passion for food. What if, at the end of each episode of *Caravan*, we had you take five minutes to talk about a recipe featuring an ingredient from one of these war zones?"

I thought about it for a few seconds and let him know that it might have been the absolute worst idea I'd ever heard. *Hey, guys, wipe those tears out of your eyes, because I'm going to tell you about some amazing things you can do with leftover cranberries!* I couldn't be a part of that.

Not one to be easily dissuaded, Amir worked hard to convince me. The war zones, he explained, were almost always Muslim countries. "We have an opportunity to highlight something positive in these places!" Sure, that was a nice sentiment, but who wants to be the "lighthearted" guy who follows a report on a *literal* war zone?

Then he tried another tack: "When was the last time you *gave back* to your Muslim community?"

Ah, see there—you're clearly barking up the wrong tree. It's quite possible that I've *never* given back to the Muslim community. I just occasionally give, and hope that the Red Cross or UNICEF or Girl Guides of Canada distribute it appropriately. At this point in my life, I still wasn't sure what kind of Muslim I was, or if I could even refer to myself as one. And while culture was becoming increasingly important, I was still that guy who once forwent the Pakistani Students' Association in favour of the Indian Students' Association. But, you know how a certain type of criminal will always leave a calling card—like a blood-curdling poem, or an ace of spades, or a pentagram—but it has their fingerprint on it? And then when they finally get caught, the cops go, "It was almost as if he *wanted* to get caught." I was reminding myself of one of those guys. *Hmm, as a caterer, he makes this Afghan appetizer; Afghanistan is a Muslim country, and right next door to Pakistan. As a comedian, he vaguely claims to be this Indo-Canadian fella, and India has the second highest population of Muslims in the world and is also right next door to Pakistan. Also, he took three years of Urdu—the national language of Pakistan—when he was at McGill University, and his parents are both Pakistani Muslims and his name is ALI HASSAN! I mean, I think we have a case here, Sarge!* My Muslim Pakistani fingerprint was on so much of what I was doing, there was no escaping that fact. I just wasn't sure how to connect with it and how to present it to others.

In the end, Amir used my own confusion against me, and guilted me into being part of this *Caravan* radio show. I reluctantly agreed that it couldn't hurt, too much, to give it a try. It turned out that Amir had spent a good amount of his lightning physicist money on audio equipment for his zero-bedroom apartment. It was small and tight, but it was a pretty impressive setup. He had three different boards with hundreds of levers and controls on them and a microphone worth $450—to my untrained eye, it seemed pretty legit. And so, in that closet/studio apartment, we started recording five-minute recipe segments to attach to the end of *Caravan*.

I enthusiastically talked about food, and Amir put his headphones on and tweaked and mastered my voice the way a true audiophile might. Per Amir's suggestion, I picked an ingredient from the Muslim world on which to focus each segment. Pomegranates to make a Syrian muhammara dip. Lemongrass for a Malaysian curry. Lemon and thyme for a Lebanese-inspired lamb roast.

Two things happened almost immediately as we started recording these segments. First, I was genuinely enjoying myself and happy to be sharing these recipes with the listeners. Second, the host of *Caravan* asked us to extend the segment from five to eight minutes. Even she—or maybe especially she—was enjoying the recipes and getting some much-needed respite from the heaviness of the show.

Around the time we had recorded our sixth episode, Amir—ever impulsive—approached me to say, "I just want to let you know that I submitted our show to CBC Radio." My reaction—my *only* possible reaction at the time—was "WHAT show? We have a five-to-eight-minute segment where I hastily offer a recipe to listeners and then maybe give them a tip on how to remove seeds from a lemon! That's not a show!" Amir maintained that we were onto something very special, and that it was worthy of our national broadcaster's attention. I shrugged my shoulders, as if to simultaneously convey a "Godspeed" and "You're a weird guy, buddy."

To my surprise (and Amir's, to be honest), a few weeks later an executive in charge of Radio Comedy at the CBC named Thomas replied. He sent an email that was succinct and included the following line: "Quite honestly, this is better than 99% of the stuff that comes across my desk."

That one line has stuck with me for years. As a creative person, you might literally wait your entire life to hear something like that from a network executive. Hearing this kind of thing should be nothing short of thrilling! My only thought, however, was *HOW SHITTY IS THIS GUY'S DESK?!* I guess you could say I was in disbelief. Thomas asked to meet with us and share more of his thoughts. This was, of course, very necessary for Amir and me, mainly to ensure we weren't part of some elaborate prank.

A few weeks later, our meeting was arranged on a date when Thomas was going to be in Montreal on other business. Amir and I met him at the CBC building, excited to learn some details, such as: our potential income, which CBC resources we would have at our disposal, and the projected time slot our brand-new hit show would occupy on national radio. It's possible that we had spent those few weeks getting a little carried away in our minds. That "better than 99%" comment can do that to a guy.

To say our meeting was brief would be an understatement:

> **Thomas:** I want to congratulate you both on this. As I mentioned in my email, I feel like you're really onto something very special here.
>
> **Amir and I:** Thank you!
>
> **Thomas:** All right, well, here's the deal. I love your work. *But,* your show, or segment as you call it, is eight minutes long. CBC Radio shows are twenty-seven minutes long. So, you've got some work to do.

Me: No problem! Let us know what you'd like to see from us
and we'll do our best to get it to you. What do we do?
Thomas: You know what? I'm not going to tell you what to
do. I think that's for you guys to figure out. And I
think you can do it.
Amir and I: (*Stunned silence.*)
Thomas: All right? Be in touch.

And with that, he left, making the roller coaster of emotions in my heart
and mind almost unbearable. I almost liked it better when I thought we were
being pranked! And all the while, I couldn't help but think that this all began
with me being convinced that I could do some good for the Muslim community at large. How was that even going to be an option going forward?

Amir and I sat back and soaked in the sobering reality that making our
radio show was going to be nowhere close to an easy process. Two things kept
us motivated at that time. First, there was a show on CBC TV titled *Little
Mosque on the Prairie* that had just began to air. The name was a play on the famous *Little House on the Prairie* show that many Canadians would have grown
up watching in the seventies and eighties, and *Little Mosque* was an absolutely
groundbreaking show, in that it centred on a Muslim community, in a prime-
time television slot. But it never had the comedic bite we wished it would.
Perhaps Amir and I could build on that. Second, we had the ear and interest
of a network executive, and as novices in this industry, we'd be damned if we
were going to squander that.

The big challenge was figuring out what the show should be. Me giving
recipes from the Muslim world just didn't seem to make sense anymore, not
for twenty-seven minutes. And particularly because we were now working with
a network radio *comedy* exec. We knew that the comedy man appreciated the
Muslim angle of our short segments, and so we set about making a half-hour
Muslim-forward radio comedy show. Easy peasy, right? God, no! For starters,
who the hell was I to be spearheading a national production that contained
Muslim content? What did I know about "Muslim comedy"? I had got into
comedy to tell jokes about food and prepare for my "eventual" food television

hosting job! I had literally *just* started to get comfortable talking about myself as a Muslim onstage. And more troublesome, how would I know if something was offensive or blasphemous? I think we can admit that the reprisals of some offended Muslims didn't just stop at a sternly-worded email. I had to defer to Amir—he was a proud practitioner of Islam and I could only hope he wouldn't lead me down the wrong path (inshallah).

Many months and many failed writing sessions later, we came up with the description of our radio show: "Muslim *Frasier* meets *The Daily Show*, followed by a recipe." It would be called *There's More to Life Than Hummus*. Yes, I'm sure that raises more questions than it answers.

If you're not familiar with the show *Frasier*, Dr. Frasier Crane was a psychiatrist who had a radio call-in show (Kelsey Grammer's Frasier character was first made famous on *Cheers* before he got his own show). Through the window of his radio booth, he often dealt with his acerbic producer, Roz. On our show, the radio show host was named Ali Hassan. I played the role of Ali Hassan, and not well. My producer was a constantly undermining, wealthy, recent immigrant from the Emirates named Abdel. I also played Abdel—somehow more convincingly than I played myself. And like *The Daily Show*, we would have guests on our call-in show. The guests were interviewees, roving reporters, and recurring columnists. And we had mock commercials. All with a light to heavy-handed Muslim spin.

The first voice-over commercial we ever made went like this: Picture light, soulful disco music playing in the background, with an uplifting beat that places the song somewhere between Chaka Khan's "I'm Every Woman" and Diana Ross's "I'm Coming Out." Good vibes. Suddenly, we hear a lady's voice—serious, almost theatrical—over the music:

> **Announcer:** Ladies, here at Cover-All International, we realize that the "he-jab" is an independent expression of your faith, your grace, and your modesty.
>
> **Background singers:** He-jab! He-jab! He-Jab!
>
> **Announcer:** But for years you have suffered with the discomfort of a hijab designed by men. But *you*

are a queen. So why not wear a product designed *by* a queen! Introducing the "she-jab"!

Background singers: She-jab! She-jab! She-Jab!

Announcer: Aerodynamic, wind tunnel tested, with pockets for your phone and lipstick. And most importantly, it's a product made for women, *by*
women. Pick up yours today. Available at all
fine, culturally sensitive retailers.

And it ended with the music stopping abruptly and a man quickly deliv-
ering the disclaimer "Product may not actually exist."

If your reaction is *"What the hell is that?!"*—you get it. You completely
understand the entire thing.

Our second mock commercial was a play on the theme of *Little Mosque*
itself. Picture this in your ears: slow Italian music plays in the background—
right out of the world of *The Sopranos*—followed by the screeching of car tires,
and some muffled gunshots in the distance. Then a scream and someone with
a deep Marlon Brando *Godfather*-esque voice saying, "You don't go behind the
family. Family is everything." A voice announcer comes on to say, "From the
creators of *Little Mosque on the Prairie . . .*" Sombre music continues and we
hear a conversation between two New Jersey–ish thugs, presumably waiting
outside in the cold for something:

Man 1: Hey, Tony, lemme axe you sometin'.

Tony: What.

Man 1: How come we never eat pepperoni?

Tony: Coz we're Muslim, stupid.

Voice Announcer: It's *Little Mosque . . .* in Little Italy. This fall on CBC.

While Amir and I may have laughed privately as we were developing
these ideas, when we heard the final product, we had to wonder: Would these
be deemed offensive? The first commercial was a tribute to the hijab, in our
minds. And the second was just an "imagine if" type of idea. If anything, it

might offend the Mafia. But these were the first things we decided to send to Thomas, to get some feedback if we were on the right track.

He wrote back that he *loved* them. And I'll never forget this: he added, "And guys, *don't be afraid to make it more Muslim.*" Neither Amir nor I knew what that meant, but we were happy that he was happy.

In our effort to develop some actual content for the show, outside of fake ads, we developed a segment with a roving reporter—a sort of pop-up that could happen at any time during the show. My friend who voiced this piece was named Faisal Butt, and we called the segment "Where in the World Is Faisal Butt?" When someone has *that* last name, you don't have to put too much work into the branding. Faisal was our own Muslim "Waldo." He would interrupt my call-in show, stranded in some faraway land, but always panting with excitement:

> **Ali:** Faisal, where are you?!
> **Faisal:** Ali, Abdel, oh my God! I'm on the beach in Jamaica.
> And you're never going to believe who I've met.
> **Ali:** Do tell!
> **Faisal:** It's the long-lost Muslim grandson of Bob Marley: Bilal Marley!
> **Ali:** Oh wow! That's very cool. What does he do?
> **Faisal:** He's a Marley, Ali. He makes music.
> **Ali:** Of course, of course. How incredible! Is he working on anything right now that he could share with us? Even a small sample?
> **Faisal** (*Muffled, speaking away from the mic*): Sorry, man, they want to know if you can do just a sample, if possible.
> **Bilal Marley:** Yeah, mon. *Ahem.*
> *I . . . drank de whis-key . . .*
> *But I did not eat de sa-la-mi . . .*
> *Oh no!*
> **Ali:** Wow! That's great, thank you, Bilal. And thank you, Faisal. Check back with us again soon!

With the mock advertisements, this sketch, and a few other items, we were up to a fifteen-minute show. But again, we needed Thomas's approval to make sure we were on the right track. We sent a file to him and heard back almost immediately. "Guys! This is exactly what I was hoping to hear! This is just terrific. Really good stuff. And again, I feel like you might be holding yourselves back, so don't be afraid to *dial up the Muslim*."

Again, we didn't really know what that meant, but his enthusiasm gave us the permission to experiment and develop more sketches, characters, and interviews. The Abdel character in particular—basically a wealthy immigrant and business owner with no filter—was morphing into someone who definitely said things that others might keep to themselves, and we constantly wondered if we were going too far. But if the national broadcaster, represented by an entire legal team, and in a constant state of concern about blowback from listeners, was giving us the thumbs-up, it gave us some confidence in our product. My self-doubt, and questions of "Am I Muslim enough to make this show?" were receding.

When we still didn't have enough to fill our twenty-seven-minute show, Amir and I came up with a movie review segment modelled after the late, great team of Siskel and Ebert. It was called "The Movie Review with Kareem and Abu." Kareem was introduced as a well-educated film studies professor who taught at Cornell University. And Abu was basically . . . an extremist. You know, that classic dynamic. It was the product of Amir and I wondering what it would sound like to have a stiff, educated Muslim and an uninformed fundamentalist Muslim in the same room.

Here's how the inaugural episode went:

> **VO** [*Over calm music*]: Welcome to *The Movie Review*, with Dr. Kareem Al-Husseini and Abu.
> **Kareem:** Good day and welcome! Today we will be looking at another incredible piece of work by director Christopher Nolan: *The Dark Knight*. This movie stars Christian Bale, Maggie Gyllenhaal, and Heath Ledger in his final performance, as Batman's nemesis, the Joker. The movie is an

epic action thriller which broke box office records. The producers decided to take the franchise into a much darker direction, eschewing previous incarnations of the epic comic book character. Incredible action, cinematography, special effects—

Abu [*Under his breath*]: Propaganda.

Kareem: Ah yes, I forgot to introduce my co-host! Abu, what are your thoughts on this great film?

Abu: It was Western propaganda.

Kareem: Ah. Okay. Well, I'm not sure I saw that—

Abu: Of course you didn't see it. You're a peasant. The Joker, he was "the bad guy," yes?

Kareem: He was.

Abu: Well, let me ask you this: What colour was the paint on the Joker's face?

Kareem: I'm . . . not one hundred percent sure. Purple, I beli—

Abu: NO. It was red, white, and green. The same colours as the Palestinian flag! HA! Coincidence? I DON'T THINK SO!

Kareem: You're being ridiculous . . .

Abu: Your mother was ridiculous!

And the music would start back up and a voiceover would calmly say, over their arguing, "You've been listening to *The Movie Review*." As soon as it ended, my producer Abdel would add, "Wow, that Kareem is very arrogant" or some thinly veiled sympathetic comment toward the extremist.

In summary, the entire thing was RIDICULOUS. But it was an absolute blast to create, and it was the edgy comedy we wanted to see in the world. We sent it all to Thomas, including a recipe (staying true to our roots) that I included for the last five minutes of the show, and a final mock commercial about a show on CBS called *CSI: MIU—Muslim Investigation Unit*. The ad promoted an episode in which a bunch of bumbling detectives barge into a Muslim florist's shop, saying they had proof in their hands that he had ordered fertilizer and uranium. The florist takes the paper and says, very calmly, "That says geraniums, and the fertilizer is for my plants. I'm a florist. Are you guys for real?" The lead detective has a moment of silence and then says, "All right, team, let's roll out!" The voice announcer ended the ad with a "This Friday on CBS, *CSI: MIU*! TGIF!" The ad, like much of the entire show, was designed to remind people that there are good, honest Muslims doing all kinds of work out there (in case you'd forgotten) and it made law enforcement look foolish. It was our little way of "sticking it to the man."

Thomas's feedback was, as always, immensely positive, and his enthusiasm for the project was undeniable. "Guys, you've really done a great job here. You have a lot to be proud of. And before you assemble it all together, if you can, don't hesitate *to sprinkle in some more Muslim.*" Okay. Whatever, man.

We finally had our full show, and Thomas scheduled a date to pitch it to his bosses. He told us to be ready around 11 a.m. on a Wednesday for a call from him, right after the pitch. Amir and I gathered at his apartment, ready to receive this call, the same way we had gathered for his original call about nine months earlier.

It felt like fate. The network had already given us a little bit of money to develop this pilot episode and hire various people to voice characters. We had already started imagining the money we would likely make from a thirteen- or twenty-six-episode season. Amir was talking about buying a car; I had been fantasizing about paying off some of my debt.

As promised, right after 11 a.m., the phone rang. Amir and I grinned uncontrollably at each other. He hit the speakerphone button.

    Thomas: Hello, gentlemen.

       Me: Thomas! Give us the news, brother!

    Thomas: Yes, well, unfortunately . . . they've decided to pass on the
            show.

      Amir: Why? What happened?

    Thomas: Well . . . they said it was "too Muslim."

For a moment, we were too bewildered to speak. *Too Muslim? Why do you think that is, Thomas? What do you think compelled us to make it so Mus-*

lim?! He told us to not get discouraged and that we could "un-Muslim" it a little bit; we could make it more of a multicultural show and resubmit it in a few months.

But we couldn't. We tried. We really did, but this show was built on a Muslim chassis. There was no taking apart the thread running directly through all of it.

I've certainly had my fair share of rejections in my life, but my reaction to that one was possibly the worst. We had worked so hard and been encouraged so much, and really put ourselves out there with the help of a number of other comedians and actors who came into Amir's apartment over the months to help us voice our cast of characters. And now it felt like it had all been for nothing, almost a year of work. And it was so hard not to take it personally. It was my first time seeing the possibility of some "success" in my professional life, and it hurt to experience another failure. Especially given how much of my heart had wound up going into this project.

But the truth was, we had no understanding of how this industry worked. How many people submit something on their first try and get an obscenely positive response from a network executive? *And* some money for a pilot episode? Almost no one, we came to realize. What I really should have felt was a tremendous amount of gratitude toward Thomas for believing in us. It took some time, but I got there.

Even though the show never got made (and let's be honest, maybe that's for the best), something incredibly positive came out of that time and work. Something truly pivotal. We had called in several local performers to help us with voices as we put together the show. In the time that Amir would be setting up the audio "booth" (two quilts over a door frame) or playing mad scientist with our audio recordings, there was a fair amount of downtime and opportunity for us performers to chat. Given that we were making a show grounded in concepts surrounding community, identity, and religion, many of our conversations went there, as well.

It so happened that during the various downtimes, two performers who were both Jewish independently and casually mentioned to me that they were "cultural Jews." I didn't know the term, or really understand it, so I probed for more info. One of them explained it to me thusly: "I'm a 'cultural Jew' in the sense that I don't believe in God, but if I have kids, I'll probably send them to Jewish school." The other performer told me that it meant he ate pork, just not on the Jewish High Holidays. This term was all over the place! And I was fascinated by it. And as I sat back and considered not just this umbrella term but also the confidence of those who aligned themselves with it, it struck me like a bag of bricks: I was a "cultural Muslim"!

This was a heavens-parting, angels-singing, lightbulb-shining moment like I had never had. My entire life I had danced around the question about my Muslim identity.

Are you Muslim? *My parents tell me I am.*
Are you Muslim? *Depends on who's asking.*
Are you Muslim? *Ehh . . . define "Muslim."*

Not only was it exhausting to do all that quick thinking, but it was also a constant reminder that I was some kind of incomplete, yet-to-be-fully-realized person. Was I eventually going to be seventy years old and still giving corny answers about my identity to people because I *still* didn't fully understand who I was? No. It turned out that, no, I wasn't. This moment of self-discovery was everything to me. Certainly, I was no practitioner of the religion. There was very little praying or mosque-attending. But it was a completely undeniable fact that everything creative that I did—from developing my catering menus, to stand-up comedy, to this insane sketch radio program—they were all rooted in my Muslim identity and background. I was, without a doubt, a cultural Muslim. And no, that wasn't even close to being a term that was in common parlance, but to hell with that. It gave me more comfort than anything I'd ever heard.

Something interesting that happens when you follow your passions, or be true to who you really are, is you start to meet the right people. By that I mean people who introduce you to new ideas that you didn't even know you were searching for. Following this path of food and comedy led me to this bizarre experiment with a CBC radio pilot, and most importantly to this epiphany.

Over the years I had used so many terms in an effort to act like I understood who I truly was. "Atheist" wasn't correct. I wanted to believe in God. I liked the idea of God. I just didn't know if God would like me very much. "Agnostic" felt like a term one came to after years of trying to determine if God existed. I had done no such research. "Non-practising Muslim" felt like I was making sure people knew there was a deliberate distance between Islam and myself. All these terms existed, and parts of them all may have even applied to me, but none ever felt comfortable. I even toyed with the idea of saying I was a "Sufi Muslim," but truthfully, I hadn't done any of the meditative and spiritual work associated with being a Sufi, so it was completely disingenuous.

As a cultural Muslim, I had done the work, and no one—not even myself—could take that away from me.

Part 5

FATHERHOOD

Chapter 19

THE ROAD TO MARRIAGE

IT WAS NEVER CLEAR if I was going to be a father. Becoming a husband seemed even less realistic. The annals of history are littered with cases of accidental fathers. But aside from the odd what-happens-in-Vegas type of trip, no one ever gets a call or letter saying, "You are the husband." *Marriage* required planning. And Faruq Hassan's son was never much of a planner. *And* I'd never been to Vegas (never mind that my overeating, excess drinking, and empty bank account had all the hallmarks of a guy who *lived* for Vegas).

My cousin Tanzeel was already planning for his eventual wedding by the age of nineteen. Some of my single friends, by their early twenties, had already mapped out the exact number and gender of children they were going to have. And I knew tons of people who had their wedding *locations* picked out. "I'm getting married on this beautiful little beach on the southern coast of Bali!" I was always left thinking, *Great! But shouldn't your partner have some say in this, or maybe even exist?* My attitude was more in the vein of "Who knows what the future holds! I certainly can't exert any control over it!"

And so, it should come as no surprise that I was still single at age thirty-five. And, in case it isn't abundantly clear by now, this wasn't a "Clooney thirty-five." I wasn't one of those highly eligible bachelors you hear about. Any woman seeking stability, financial prowess, and a full head of hair in her mate would have to keep walking.

On paper, I should have relished the idea of getting married. South Asians love their weddings. It's a time to dance, drink, and eat. What's not to love?

Pakistanis—particularly those under the more sobering influence of Islam—will put a little less emphasis on the dancing and much less on the drinking. But that still leaves the food.

The DJ could be good, or not. There could be a dance floor, or not. The bride and groom could be in love, or not. But goddamn you, your food better be delicious, or we will remember this lowlight for the rest of our lives. When I say "we," I'm actually not even talking about myself. Despite my love of food, I was able to suspend the needs of my "sophisticated palate" when the chef was cooking for five hundred. Maybe because of my own restaurant and catering experience, I had mercy on the kitchen staff and quickly lowered my expectations.

Not my family, though. I remember attending one particularly lavish wedding where the groom trotted in on a gorgeous white horse—he and the animal were both decorated in Indian regalia as a live band played music around him. Throughout the night, there were three different dance performances, each more elaborate and professional than the last. And the food was all separated by various regions in India, served at five different "stations": Punjab, Mumbai Street Food, Kerala, Tamil Nadu, and Bengal. It was sensational. On our way home, as my dad unbuttoned his pants in the car and my ears rang from dancing too close to a speaker for two and a half hours, my mother offered this one comment: "The rice was a bit dry."

Come on, Mom! FIVE food stations for hundreds of guests—think of all the work that went into that! And the rehearsals required for those incredibly well-choreographed dances? And the groom, who must have taken hours to get adorned like an Indian four-star general, and his badass horse? He probably needed horse-riding lessons for that all to go so smoothly! What must happen at a wedding for you to forget about the moisture level of the rice?

There was one *actual* problem with the wedding: the couple discovered in the *very* moment the groom trotted in that the bride had an asthmatic allergy to horses. The groom had been on the horse for so long, that as far as her allergies were concerned, there was no difference between him and the horse. There was a pretty-rough thirty minutes of her wheezing outside, before the groom was finally instructed to go home, shower thoroughly, and change into something else.

By the time I was in my mid-thirties, I was finding South Asian weddings, not unlike the rice on that fateful night, increasingly dry. And I don't mean absent of alcohol. I don't *just* mean absent of alcohol. Between attending and catering, I had spent a lot of time at a *lot* of weddings. And they weren't bad per se. But sitting through the actual receptions had become painful. I'm referring primarily to what was happening on the mic. While my community was busy with their forensic audits of the food, my focus was locked on what was transpiring on that microphone. All I ever wanted was a good MC and someone with a decent wedding speech. Was that too much to ask? It just might have been.

The recycled material that some of the uncles were bringing to the podium was wearing me down. "Sameena, put out your hand. Now, Muneeb, put your hand on top of Sameena's hand. Muneeb, this is the last time you will ever have the upper hand! HAHAHAHAHA!"

Uncle, I actually want to strangle you for thinking that is funny for the five hundredth time. And why are the guests laughing? I've seen most of you at every other wedding this summer, where someone else told this exact same joke!

I'd also been listening to hundreds of speeches from friends of the brides and the grooms. Words like "destiny" and "soul mate" were being thrown around with a pretty loosey-goosey interpretation; it's hardly "kismet" that some aunty knew the bride's family and the groom's family and, in her quest for Cupid's high, thought to set the couple up. I'm not made of stone— these speeches were touching at first, but eighteen years of attending several weddings a year will break anyone. Most of the speeches left me thinking, *A lot of this could have just been written in a card and handed directly to the couple.* Unsentimental? Sure, I've been called worse.

At the end of the day, it was probably a lot of projection and distraction on my part. *Oh, when am I getting married?* Never mind that, why is the bridesmaid telling five hundred guests inside jokes about a summer camp we've never heard of?! While I may have been relegating myself to a life of eternal bachelordom, my relatives most certainly didn't see things that way. In South Asian communities, a single thirty-five-year-old man is cause for widespread panic. The days of "concern" were five years prior. At this point, we were in proper panic mode. Pakistani parents have what I call the Stages of Matrimonial Panic when it comes to their son's nuptials.

> When you are in your twenties: "Your wife should be a
>   Muslim Pakistani."
> Once you hit thirty: "Son, she could be Shia Muslim or Sunni
>   Muslim—we are very open-minded about such things."
> At thirty-two, a global approach begins: "She can be from any
>   Muslim country—Kenyan, Indonesian. We don't want to lock
>   you in."
> At thirty-four: "You know, any bloody woman will do at this
>   point. Any religion, any colour. Just get married. Please."

And then, you're thirty-five. There's just one last-ditch effort to make.

But before I get into that matrimonial Hail Mary, here's some information for you to chew on: My parents were first cousins. I'm sorry, there's really no gentle way to say that. And if that's a little jarring for you to read, imagine how I felt when I found out.

That wasn't a great day. I was about fourteen years old, having recently learned the risks involved in incestual unions. I was, in fact, making fun of them at the dinner table.

> "George Bush looks like someone you get when two cous-
>   ins get married, right, Mom?"
> Awkward pause. "You know, your father and I are first cousins."
> "I'm sorry, Mother, but this mutton biryani doesn't taste very
>   good anymore. May I be excused?"

I know, I know—many a wonderful, loving, lasting marriage has come from cousins who got married back in the old country. But I considered myself very "new country." I even considered my parents "new country" (I realize it sounds like I'm talking about a radio station in small-town Alberta). My dad held so many progressive views on so many subjects; my mother and her sister lived in New York City in their late teens and twenties; her brother, Shahyar, was a jiu-jitsu master; her father had gotten remarried to a white British woman; my mother's youngest sister, Tamzin, had married our Belgian uncle Daniel—I mean, we were cool, right? We were worldly, no? My Canadian identity was rattled. Particularly because I hadn't picked up on this bit of alarming news earlier in life.

My first real question, when I recovered from the shock, was "Isn't that dangerous?" My mother replied, "Not for first cousins, one time. But, for example, it wouldn't be safe for *you* to marry a cousin." "Oh good. Yes, *that's* why I won't do it, because of your safety concerns." But at least I knew my mother wasn't ever going to push me toward any of my cousins, right? RIGHT?

And so, back to my parents' last-ditch effort to marry off their thirty-five-year-old son. My mother called me on the phone one day, her voice sounding a little sweeter than normal.

"Ali, do you remember Seema? She's a nice girl. She comes from a good family. In fact, you know the family. It's *our* family."

Her real name isn't Seema. Strangers are reading this and I'm not a monster. But consider the fact that my parents, who are cousins, were now trying to convince me to also consider marrying a cousin. "But she's not your *first* cousin," my mother kept trying to remind me, "she's a distant cousin." To me, it was akin to "Smoke this crack. It's not pure crack. It's pretty diluted crack!" Call me crazy but I just don't like my mother forcing me to smoke crack, however distilled it might be.

They were desperate, and the sales pitch was strong:

She's in Toronto. You could move there and find a good job.
She has a good job. She could help support your comedy "career."
She has a big extended family—they could help raise your children.

Yes, my possibly hunchbacked, ogre children, who are the products of multiple generations of cousins getting married. I was dead set against it. It angered my mother to no end, and she was prepared with counterarguments.

"Twenty percent of all couples across the world are cousins!"

"Okay, Mom, but we know better."

"So, it's gross if it's Pakistanis, but acceptable when it was the British monarchy? Victorian England was *filled* with kissing cousins!"

"Have you taken a good look at the monarchy? There are some weird-looking people in that mix. Prince Charles married Diana for a reason!"

"Albert Einstein married his first cousin."

"Mom, as you yourself have told me many times, I'm no Einstein."

I actually went to meet her, this distant cousin. That might sound surprising, but my aunt and uncle were putting a lot of pressure on me. My father wasn't well, and wouldn't live forever, and my aunt made sure to inject that into my head. "Your father's last wish is for you to get married before he dies!" Powerful negotiators, these relatives of mine. And possibly liars, as well.

We went to meet her at her family home. My aunt, on the doorstep of the house, jabbed me in the ribs and whispered in Punjabi: "*Akhaan khol ke vekho*," which means "Open your eyes and look properly," but in a stronger tone than the words suggest. I did open my eyes, and I did look properly. And I saw a cousin. She was a nice girl. A lovely girl, even. But my answer, despite the pleas and "last wishes," was no.

I only later realized that this time in my life had left an emotional scar. Even to this day when people ask me, "How did you meet your wife?" my first instinct is to defensively claim, "*She's not my cousin, okay?!*"

When I finally did meet my wife, I did things the old-fashioned way. You know the story: you meet somebody special, but you don't have much to offer in the way of security, success, or potential, so you chicken out and wait too long and they marry someone else. Then you wait for them to have a daughter. And then you wait a little longer, long enough for them to have a second daughter. And then you bide your time, waiting for them to get divorced . . . and *then*, when you feel like you still really don't have that much to offer, at age thirty-six, you finally ask them out.

The very first time I met my wife-to-be, I was in my twenties, and it was thanks to an introduction from her older sister, Farah. Farah was a friend from McGill and thought her younger sister and I might just hit it off. She wasn't wrong! We met outside by the bus station in Toronto—we were gathered to see off Farah as she headed back to Montreal. Farah's sister was wearing a royal-blue matching-top-and-bottom tracksuit that day, and she was a clubhead. That is, she was often at nightclubs dancing her heart out, courtesy of her friend who was a DJ.

Now, since that day, my wife has sworn that she never owned a matching track outfit, or even anything royal blue. She admits she *may* have frequented nightclubs, but doesn't really care for dancing. Which begs the question, who *was* that girl I met?

In any case, I know that I did indeed meet her and my first thought was *God, she's lovely.* Then I looked at myself and thought, *Don't nobody need none of this right now.* My MBA program had just wished me better luck in my future endeavours (of which none were forthcoming), I was thoroughly in debt, and had absolutely no idea about what to do next with my life.

And so, almost fifteen years later, settling down with my non-cousin wife, who I met without the help of any of my relatives, felt pretty good to me. And she arrived with gifts: those two daughters that I mentioned. Marrying a woman with kids is an interesting thing. First, one must endure many well-intentioned friends and relatives saying things like "You're a good man. Personally, I'm not sure if I could ever marry a woman with that kind of baggage." Hey, here's a thought, maybe referring to my kids-to-be as "baggage" isn't really helping anyone. Second, one inevitably has personal insecurities about being a father that they must overcome. It was a pretty hard right turn from being a single dude, dancing my ass off at after-hours clubs, to being a married man entrusted with taking his brand-new children to the Royal Agricultural Winter Fair for an equestrian show.

But they were the sweetest, most precious kids I'd ever met. I was scared that *I* would be the problem. That I wouldn't do right by them. I worried that they didn't deserve a degenerate like me as a dad. But what I learned very quickly is that degeneracy is all relative. Granted, my income was still pitiful. It came from $12/head catering gigs and beer tickets from open-mic comedy shows; that is to say, my finances were fuelled by dreams and passion. In a partnership, maybe you can afford to dream. But if you're going to be a father, you should at least provide, no? It turned out, the girls' biological dad—I'll spare you the gory details—provided even less than I did. And he was much higher on the degeneracy ladder than I was. Or is it lower on the ladder? Anyway, he was the bad one. Relative to him, I appeared to be a saint and a saviour.

I steadied myself and settled in for a long, fruitful life of being a father to two girls. We didn't plan to have more children—you know me and planning—but it wasn't off the table, either. Honestly, my wife wasn't much more of a planner and we literally had this conversation.

> **Her:** Would you want to have another kid?
> **Me:** I don't know. Would *you* want to have another kid?
> **Her:** I guess I wouldn't *not* want to have another kid. If you don't.
> **Me:** Okay, look, I was raised in a house that didn't allow double
> negatives. I don't really know what's going on right now. Are
> we going to have sex, or what?

And so, with that precise level of strategizing in place, my wife found out she was somehow pregnant, two months after our wedding. I say "somehow" because I certainly didn't think *I* had anything to do with it! After decades of drinking, a lifetime of consuming nothing but artery-clogging foods, and not to mention all the long car rides with my cell phone tucked between my inner thighs, how could this happen?

I was happy to have another child; happy that the girls would have a little brother. He would need to know rather soon that his grandparents on his dad's side were cousins and that he'd probably never be an elite athlete. Also, his hair and teeth would be doomed, and he wouldn't get much of a religious education. But other than that, the world could be his oyster. Three years later, my wife was pregnant again. In four years, I amassed four children. "Amass" isn't the right word—it sounds like I purchased them on the black market. More to the point, I went from a single man to a father of four very quickly. On paper, any father in my position should have been freaking out. Sole income earner, in an unpredictable industry, with five mouths to feed (six, if you count me, and I definitely did), and no real experience in, or talent for, parenting. I sat back and waited for the panic to set in. It never came.

Early on, my wife and the girls may have seen me as some sort of saviour, but the truth is, they saved me. Not only that, but I'd even say that marriage is the thing that keeps me most grateful and most connected to God—as in, I thank God pretty much daily for making it such that my wife and I could reconnect and marry. Regardless of how or when we met, the weird and winding roads that we took to each other, it's all worked out (and with absolutely no thanks to my parents' attempts at matchmaking). I guess you could say I owe my wife's first husband a debt I'll never be able to repay. There's something you don't hear every day.

Chapter 20

ISLAM IN THE HASSAN HOUSEHOLD

THE PENIS IS AN INTERESTING THING. Not in the way it looks, perhaps. In that regard, it's a hilarious thing. But for me, I can't think about fatherhood, or Islam, without thinking about the penis.

A decade ago, I was as clueless about the procedure of a vasectomy as I was about a hysterectomy or cataract removal. I knew vasectomies were performed on men, to ensure they didn't have children—that's it. If you told me the surgery involved a cement truck backing up to your bedroom window and pouring concrete onto your lap, I might have believed you. So, the thought that I might one day need one certainly never crossed my mind. If anything, I would have thought I may need the opposite: a procedure that finds all your dead sperm and, using some kind of semen defibrillator, shocks it all back to life (thinking I might patent this process, just in case).

But after the announcement of our fourth child, and a general unease in my wife's eyes every time I approached her, it was clear that I was going to need to investigate this thing. My reckless sperm knew nothing about my finances or my child-rearing capacity—they had gone rogue, and something needed to be done.

A vasectomy is one of those things that no one really talks about, but once I quietly suggested that I was "perhaps in the market" for one, I heard the most enthusiastic chorus of "I got a guy!" from dozens of male friends, and "We got a guy!" from their wives. One hears that line throughout their life, but usually the "guy" is an accountant, or mechanic, or butcher. I suppose it makes sense—if you're keen to refer others to the pro who saves you money, changes your oil, or wraps your salami, it stands to reason the person who does something considerably more unnerving should also come highly recommended.

In the end, I had been referred to so many "guys" that I chose to just do my own research. I didn't want to be in a position of thinking to myself, *Zach's doctor messed things up! Why didn't I go with the guy who did Tara's husband?* This was no time for buyer's remorse! If there were going to be any mistakes, they were going to be on me. On me, literally, and also because of me, but courtesy of a stranger with a medical degree.

I called a clinic I liked the look of and they sent me the various pertinent details. When I called back a few weeks later to book an appointment, the receptionist went over the openings in the schedule and named the *three* doctors who were working that week. This came as a surprise—I now had three penis doctors. I don't think that's their official name, but I was still learning.

Now I had a choice. Do I google "Vasectomies gone wrong," accompanied by each doctor's name, or do I just go with my gut? The latter was less work, so I went with that, but it appears that my gut might just be a racially motivated organ. Out of the three, I chose the doctor with the clearly Jewish name. Now, before you label this as discrimination, keep in mind two things. First, I was entrusting myself *to* this man, not casting him out. And second, Jewish people, in my experience, have a lot of words for "penis." Between Yiddish and Hebrew, I've heard dozens over the years. *Putz, schmuck, schmeckle, shtrunkle, pickle*—there are a lot! If you'll allow the generalization, they seem pretty interested in "the region." It felt like a good fit.

When the day came and I met the doctor, he seemed lovely. He told me that he actually worked full-time in palliative care but picked up shifts in the vasectomy world because it was something more hopeful and tangibly helpful than his everyday work. He went on to explain that too much time doing exclusively palliative work was tough on a doctor's mental health—but my mind had wandered to the fact that he only had part-time experience in the matter at hand.

Trust me—when one discovers that one's penis doctor is not technically a penis doctor, it is disconcerting. But I buried all my fears deep down inside. Things got less easy to bury when he asked what I did. I told him I was a stand-up comedian, and he replied, "No way! That's terrific! Comedy is a hobby of mine!"

Look, I think it's great to bond with a doctor before a procedure, I really do. But I don't want to know about my doctor's hobbies at a time like this. I want to think that my doctor has one focus in life, and that is my penis. Also, is this the best time for comedy? Women will rightfully scoff at this and call me a huge baby, but for a man, this is possibly the most vulnerable position you can be in (albeit prostate exams are sure to change all that). You lie on a table, with your pants off, legs open, surrendering the future of your best friend to a stranger. Is this the time to hear a joke? What if I laugh and my body jiggles? There should be no jiggling during a procedure like this! Or what if the joke is terrible? And I'm left staring at the ceiling, wondering if my doctor is also bad at the other, arguably more important thing he is here to do?!

He told me his favourite comedian was Rodney Dangerfield and proceeded to tell me some Rodney-style jokes that he loved doing with his male patients. This is the one that stuck with me most. As he was hunched over my testicles, putting on his reading glasses to examine them in great in detail, he looked up at me and said, "My job, I tell ya, my job is tough. Oh, it's tough all right. Every day, I gotta go to work with a prick and two nuts. Nurse, scalpel!"

The joke is one that I've heard and read before over the years, but what struck me most was how he turned his head to the left and said, "Nurse, scalpel!" There was no nurse. In fact, there was no one else in the room. Also, it was a scalpel-free procedure. He just yelled those words to a blank wall. I was actually impressed by his commitment. And luckily, he also went deep in character as a urologist that day, and his work was—and remains to this day—a success.

The whole event got me thinking more about religion and the penis. I have always felt that in a man's quest to establish once and for all if he is really a Muslim, the final battleground is circumcision. It is where the struggle for

Muslim identity truly reaches a head (no pun intended). When all the dust has settled, the question "Are you a Muslim or not?" is solved in the realm of the foreskin. If you're a *Star Trek* fan, we're talking about *Foreskin: The Final Frontier*. If Shakespeare is more your thing: To snip or not to snip, *that* is the circumcision.

What I mean by all this is that if someone born into the Islamic faith opts to drink alcohol and eat pork, they *could* still be a Muslim. If they don't pray, they could still be a Muslim. But if you ever meet someone who opts not to circumcise their son? That is a person who has truly disconnected from their faith. And if you were to look at the penises of my sons—God willing, you won't—you will see that I am indeed still a Muslim.

That said, it's truly an awful thing to go through for a parent. Yeah, I guess the kid suffers a bit, too. And by the way, this chapter won't have any accompanying photos—I think it's fair of me to let you know that ahead of time. Just go into your mind and envision the worst thing you could voluntarily ask a doctor to do to your male child in the Western world. We did that.

My first memory of this doctor (yes, again Jewish) was that he was late! And the same guy was also late three and a half years later when we did the same thing to my second son. I remember these things because every moment that your circumcision doctor is late creates more anxiety for parents—especially those who are engaging in a ritual with a minor risk of complication and a hundred percent risk of bleeding and screaming. The procedure has a real "Just get it over with" vibe to it. But what could I possibly say to the doctor? I mean, he's really got the upper hand here—you don't want to criticize the punctuality of the man who has your son's penis in his hands. Ten years later, you don't want to have this conversation:

"Papa, why does my penis look like a fork?"
"Well, kiddo, Papa felt it was important to scold the doctor performing your circumcision, to teach him that he should be more considerate of other people's schedules. I guess he didn't take kindly to that. Let me just say, again, I am sorry that your pee sprays out like a garden sprinkler."

In any case, both times, the procedures were done "successfully." It's the small victories that count in a situation like this. You'd think the worst part was the actual cutting. You'd be wrong. The worst part is most certainly when your son looks up at you and his innocent, three-week-old face says, "WHY? Why would you do this to me?" I'm not sure why, buddy. I'm a little confused about this myself. The health reasons are out the window. I don't practise the religion enough for this to matter. It was done to me—for free, in a hospital that did it routinely unless you asked for it not to be done—and so maybe I needed to spend $270 and "pay" it forward?

If I'm being honest, it's because I'm a Muslim. My sons, you'll have penises that are slightly shorter than those of your white friends' penises, and a little less sensitive to the touch, because your father is a Muslim. And so are you.

Maybe that's enough? Surely my connection to Islam through culture, food, art, ten years of Sunday school, and the two circumcisions performed in my family with my "blessing" all suggest that I am a Muslim! Unfortunately, a quick chat about religion with my children will cast all of that in doubt.

A few years ago, when my daughters were eleven and thirteen, and my older son was five, I was recording a piece for a CBC Radio program called *Tapestry*. The show "explores spirituality, religion, and the search for meaning." I had been loaned a voice recorder and decided to start by talking to my own children. Three of them, anyway. The fourth one was around, he was just more of an angry yeller and a shrieker at that time.

I began with my five-year-old.

"What do Muslims believe in?"
"You can't eat pork."
"Okay, that sounds accusatory. What else?"
"Umm . . . Jesus?"
"Okay . . . sure. [*Silence.*] Anyone else?"
"The Prophet Muhammad?"

To be fair, Muslims *do* believe that Jesus existed; they believe he was a prophet of God. But the fact that my son brought up Jesus's name first was a bit of a surprise. And the fact that both Jesus and Muhammad's names were followed by question marks was a concern.

I guess that between my desire for my children to learn how to cook for themselves, swim, unclog a toilet, snag ground balls, and take music lessons, religion just doesn't come up much. But after "interviewing" them, I realized it really didn't come up at all.

When I was young, myself and all the kids around me seemed to have some basic knowledge about religion. Sure, I may have actively resisted learning a lot of it because of my own issues with Arabic and Sunday school, but I knew stuff. And we also had religious instruction in school. I had a class throughout high school called MRE (Moral and Religious Education). Yes, it was taught by the gym teacher, but we *had* it. And my wife was at a Catholic school. And people just talked about God and religion more often.

But now, with religion being a no-go zone in high schools and many conversations, my kids know nothing and it's a source of some anxiety for my wife and me. Religion is an important part of world history. And of our family's histories. Even if it isn't necessarily a clear part of our future.

At one point in my *Tapestry* preparation, I asked my daughters how many times a day a Muslim is supposed to pray. They both said "five," but with so much doubt and trepidation that the answer didn't even count as correct. And here's something that was never added to the interviews. I just heard it and buried it deep down for a few years.

My thirteen-year-old was struggling to figure out what to do for her birthday when, exasperated, she asked at the dinner table: "Why can't I have a bar mitzvah?!" My thirteen-year-old *Muslim daughter* asked why she couldn't have a *bar mitzvah*. And before I could answer, my eleven-year-old laughed at her and said, "We're *not* Mexican!" SIGH. Mixing up her bar mitzvahs with her quinceañeras. On which you must be *quince* años. FIFTEEN. What a mess.

I always believed in the existence of God. I still do. Although now my understanding of God is not a He or a She or even a supreme "being," but more of an energy. If you put out a good energy and do good things, good energy comes your way.

The *practise* of religion is something I stopped seeing the value in a long time ago. And I have no guilt about that. I am comfortable in my own skin and very content being this "cultural Muslim." But the problem now is these kids! *They* aren't the problem, to be clear, but they have me wondering if we need some solution to their knowledge gap.

It's not in schools unless you send them to religious school—and then you only really learn about one religion because apparently all the others suck. It's certainly not available to my five-year-old. I often think that the idea of a heaven and a hell might help my kids apply a checks-and-balances system to their behaviour. God is not unlike Santa Claus—making a list, checkin' it twice, that type of thing. The difference of course is, with Santa, if you're bad you don't get a gift. With God, if you're bad, you live out your eternity in the fires of hell. The point is, try to be good!

Do I need to host weekly religious seminars just to get them "up" to the unimpressive knowledge that I have? Clearly, some outsourcing would be required. "And now we have a special guest at our seminar today to talk about Catholicism—it's . . . your mom! And later on, to share stories about the Prophet Muhammad that your father doesn't remember because he was zoned out in Sunday school—you know her, you love her . . . it's Grandma!"

However we do this, I want them to discover religion—or at the very least, their spiritual side. Because even if one day they feel that organized religion is too difficult, or a sham, or just not for them, shouldn't they at least have some connection to a spiritual side? I hate to think that their lives, down the line, are less fulfilling because they were never introduced to some basic divine concepts.

Islamic education in the Hassan household is a moving target. The girls are old enough now that they've got this stuff straight (not much thanks to me). And the boys may not know much yet, but at least they are circumcised. The door to religion or spirituality (or whatever) will always be open to them.

Chapter 21

TEACHINGS/LEARNINGS

MY FATHER-IN-LAW LIKES TO WATCH CNN on volume level 47 out of 50, so every trip to Grandpa's is quite educational, whether we want it to be or not. In late 2015, Donald Trump was campaigning and building significant support for his run at the American presidency. His modus operandi was to frequently rely on divisive and racist commentary. Earlier that year he had already linked Mexican immigrants to rapists, and now he was talking about the need for surveillance of American mosques and American Muslims themselves.

One day at Grandpa's, in December 2015, my then ten-year-old daughter heard Donald Trump—loudly and clearly—call for "a total and complete shutdown of Muslims entering the United States" until the country could "figure out what is going on." This comment was connected to a particularly awful mass shooting by a Muslim married couple in San Bernardino, California, but what he was really doing was engaging in some on-brand fearmongering. To that end, Trump went on to speak about his proposed Muslim ban and a call for a registry. My daughter turned to me and asked, "What's a registry?"

Not an ideal conversation to have with your child, certainly. I explained that it was *probably* (what the hell did I really know about this plan!) some kind of list or repository that keeps track of the whereabouts and behaviour of Muslims. That idea immediately made her uncomfortable, and in a panic, she asked me, "Are we weird? Are Muslims weird?" "No! No, we aren't weird. Donald Trump is weird!"

But the truth is, we *are* weird. We are *all* weird. As I later told my daughter, don't think you can leave *this* weird, looking for *no* weird, because every family and community has its weird. And every religion is a complex system that has some variation of weirdness. It really comes down to timing. If any major religion started today, we'd all be pointing at it and saying, "Look at that bizarre cult!" Who knows—if Scientology were a thousand years old, most of us might have been praying to Lord Cruise right now.

I'm certain there are people—predominantly white people—reading this right now, saying to themselves, "Well, thankfully we aren't weird." Let me just squash that right now, in case you're one of them. The rest of the world thinks you do things that are pretty darn weird. *Like what?* Well, here's a short list:

1. Wearing outdoor shoes inside the house.
2. Referring to black pepper as a spice.
3. Letting your daughter's teenage boyfriends sleep over.
4. Putting milk in your green tea.
5. Dinner at 5 p.m.?
6. Travelling to India to "find yourself."

Ultimately, we are all doing things that others will consider weird. But I think the important thing is doing the hard work to just accept that about each other. And even celebrate it. I often think about this fact: Plenty of Westerners make fun of the country of Pakistan, or at the very least have found it to be weird on multiple levels. But I can't accept that. Not when parts of America today have become *exactly* like the Pakistan that my father left fifty years ago. The influence that the conservative religious community holds, the corruption, the disregard for the common folk from industry and government, the failure of the education system, the unchecked power of the military, violence against minority groups—I mean, looking at this list, it's impossible to tell which country I am even talking about! And sadly, our beloved Canada is similar to the US in so many ways. We may get off on judging others, but at some level, sooner or later, we'll all have our own weird shit, too.

Courtesy of Donald Trump, I had to sit my children down and explain to them that they didn't need to worry about their identity. Being Muslim wasn't a scary or unfortunate predicament they found themselves in. I pointed at the fact that a man named Naheed Nenshi was the Muslim mayor of Calgary at the time. Calgary—the largest city in a province that was once nicknamed "the Texas of the North." Pakistani Brit Sadiq Khan was elected the mayor of London, and at the very same time that England was starting its Brexit campaign. And, oddly, my kids didn't need to look any further than their own father's career: a Muslim dude hired by the national public broadcaster *because* he was Muslim, because the CBC wanted a diverse voice on a comedy panel. My first job at the network, as a virtual unknown, was on a TV show called *George Stroumboulopoulos Tonight* as the lead comedy panelist—thanks to George himself, in large part. From there I moved into radio, hosting nationally broadcast shows, and the work continued. My background was never an issue.

Actually, that's not entirely true. I once got a call from a television producer I knew, asking me if I was still interested in hosting food television shows. I told him I was, and he was excited to tell me about a brand-new show concept he was going to pitch me for, called *Fly Me to the Food*. He eagerly shared all the details: "So, you know how major international airports have now become a home to great restaurants, owned by celebrity chefs, right? Like you can finally get great meals in hundreds of airports across the world! Well, in this show, a host—and I think you'd be so perfect for this—travels to all these airports and interviews the chefs and customers at all these top-notch eating establishments! Whaddyathink?"

I absolutely loved the idea, but there was an elephant in the room, and I had to mention it. "This is great, but have you given it some thought, this idea of *me* being the host?" He was baffled—"Of course! What do you mean?" "Well, you've given some thought to the idea of your host being a guy named Ali Hassan, who travels from airport to airport, from airplane to airplane, clearing customs as he goes from country to country . . . I mean, *I* love it. But you're sure it won't be an issue for anyone?" He paused ever so slightly and said, "Not at all!" and then immediately followed up with "Hey, I have to take this call. I'm going to call you right back!" That was in 2008—I never heard from him again. On the one hand, it was so sweet that he never even considered that

Ali Hassan might delay production while he sat in secondary screening. On the other hand, it had to be addressed, and if it hadn't been me, someone was certainly going to do it down the line.

So, not every job needs and wants Ali Hassan as a host, and that's perfectly fine. But as I explained to my children, for every few organizations that don't want you around, there will be at least one that does. And that's the one you should want to work for, too. The point, I tried to hammer home, was to focus on the positive. Even when things seemed to look bleak for Muslims, there was positive stuff all around us.

When I search my name today on Google, I am often the first Ali Hassan that comes up. This doesn't impress my children—their job as my children is not to be impressed by their father—but I hope *you're* impressed! That is like being the first John Smith that comes up on the internet! Or maybe Ron Smith. John is more like Muhammed Hassan. And I share that top spot periodically with another Ali Hassan, an actor from India. And I will tell you why that doesn't bother me one bit: a decade ago, when I used to type in Ali Hassan, I had to click through five or so pages of Middle Eastern politicians, various criminals like "Chemical Ali" and the "Butcher of Baghdad," and even a sheepherder in Yemen before I got to me. And what does a sheepherder need a web page for, anyway?

When I toured my comedy show *Muslim, Interrupted*, for four years, from 2016 to 2019, it was described as "a funny, socially poignant show that strives to counter the tide of hatred and Islamophobia that exists globally and in this country." So, I look at it like this: if my name, or any other comedian, actor, or singer, or even potter of the same name pops up well before any of the Ali Hassans of ill repute, this can only be good news for all of us. I was always bad at physics, but there's one axiom that has certainly stayed with me: for every action, there is an equal and opposite reaction. There might be calls for bans and registries, but there is also demand for the hard work and talent of many Muslims in many fields.

A few decades ago, in my late teens, I was doing something I did quite often (no, not that, you perverts): I was perusing my dad's extensive library of books. Sitting somewhere between a literary criticism on James Joyce and the collected works of Pakistani writer Saadat Hasan Manto, I found a transcript of an interview with my father. It was in an issue of a local Indo-Canadian magazine, which that month was featuring an interview with "Montreal writer, poet and professor, Faruq Hassan."

The interviewer was asking my father about creativity and commenting on how ideal the job of teaching literature must be for a writer and a poet. My father replied that it actually sapped him of his creative energies. The interviewer then asked my father if having children affected his creativity, and his answer was something to the effect of "Absolutely. Children kill creativity. Creativity requires time, and children take that time away from you." The message was pretty clear: Dad would have been a more productive writer if he'd been a childless banker.

Looking back, it feels like that was something I should have never read. Reading comments like that as a younger man can breed resentment. Like "Oh, your *kids* kill creativity? What about the fifteen to twenty hours a week you spend with your buddies? Is that some kind of a weekly, Labatt-sponsored writers' conference?"

More importantly, his answer in that interview transcript seemed to be delivered with such conviction that I assumed it had to be true of all creatives. I almost used it as a crutch as I got older: "Yeah, I'm still single. Probably for the best, because if I ever get married and have children, they will affect the quality of all my work." I heard similar sentiments echoed by others over the years, including the owner of a comedy club I worked at, when he found out I was going to marry a woman who had two children already.

But as a father of four, I have found myself in complete disagreement with my father and all those who might identify with his comment. My children have made me *more* creative. Perhaps because of their curiosity and inquisitive natures, or maybe because when you see hungry mouths in front of you, you say to yourself, "I better get to work so I can feed these people." I've never articulated that to myself before, but I'm sure it's always existed in the back of my mind somewhere.

In 2008, early in my career, I was invited to perform at the Amman Comedy Festival. I'm still not sure why or how it happened, but it remains one of the greatest experiences of my comedy career. More memorable than the comedy even was a luncheon we had with the mayor of Amman, the afternoon before the festival started. As I sat in a room with Maz Jobrani, Aron Kader, Dean Obeidallah, Russell Peters, and many other established and hilarious comedians, wondering what I'd done to deserve this gift, the mayor addressed us all and spoke solemnly: "On behalf of the King and Queen, myself and my team, I want to thank you all for bringing laughter to a region so desperately in need of it." In that moment, I realized that comedy was so much more than standing in a club and telling jokes. Comedy had power and it had potential. I was just too young in the industry to know what that potential was. Now I believe I'm aware of at least some of that potential, and my hope is to challenge preconceived notions and long-standing biases and prejudices through humour. And most of all, my hope is that, in my own way, I will remind people that we all have more similarities than differences.

It's not an exaggeration to add that my children *made* my career. All I have is because of them. And, of course, my wife, who stepped up to spend the lion's share of time with the kids—time they absolutely require. My father-in-law, not a creative man by his own admission, has a different perspective on children. He likes to say, "Every child brings its own luck." I don't know if that's true for everyone, but it's as clear as day that as my family has grown, my luck and my opportunities have grown. Quite simply, perhaps too many single, creative men were behaving like absolute monsters, and this father of four has seemed like a stable, risk-averse hiring choice, if even for a night. Or maybe given my own upbringing, or the years that I seemed destined to be a lifelong bachelor, I'm able to look at fatherhood—most days, anyway—as an absolute gift. Many years ago, when I would taste the food I was making for my customers, I was confident that if I enjoyed it, they were going to enjoy it, too. In the same way, I know that when I'm doing work I love and am proud of, it's something my children can be proud of, too.

Chapter 22

THE 06 CULTURAL MUSLIM

MY DAD WASN'T TYPICAL OF his generation of Pakistani Canadians. Many of the members of that first wave of immigration in the late 1960s and '70s had backgrounds in the sciences and pursued jobs as engineers and doctors. My dad made a career out of his devotion to English and Urdu literature and encouraged generations of young people in Montreal to appreciate the best work in both languages.

While many of those same early wave immigrants turned to a dogmatic form of Islam as they aged, my father never deviated from a more humanistic Sufi Islam—one that focused more on an intensely personal form of spirituality. Throughout his life, my dad eschewed Islamic piety and fanaticism. Despite, or maybe because of, that time in Saudi Arabia, he remained devoted to the liberalism and free thought necessary for literature to thrive.

Despite the drinking, he always said he was a Muslim. He might have held many negative views on various Muslim "leaders" and politicians, but he never bad-mouthed God or people who practised the religion. He simply avoided them. And then I found out that he was sending some money every year to that pir—a revered spiritual guide who would essentially listen to people's problems and say prayers for them—in his hometown in Pakistan. If you can believe it, it occurred to me only as I was writing this book that my dad was the quintessential cultural Muslim.

I mentioned earlier that to pressure me into finding someone, *anyone*, to marry, my family guilted me by saying my father wouldn't be around forever.

There was actually more to that. He had been diagnosed with pulmonary fibrosis years earlier; it is a chronic lung condition, and he'd been given only a few years to live. My father passed away in 2011, after a year of rapidly deteriorating health, and just a few weeks after meeting and holding my first son. It always gave me comfort that a man who lived a hard and fast life, and whose first love was tobacco, still made it to seventy-two, old enough to see that his wayward son was going to have a family, and maybe—hopefully—be all right.

Dad's second love might have been a good laugh, and I'm certain he would have gotten a kick out of the absurdity of trying to arrange his funeral. I've learned a funny thing about funerals. They don't always go as planned.

The day he passed away, we called the mosque. There's no easy way into that discussion, so I just dove right in: "Hello, I'm calling to make arrangements for my father, who passed away a few hours ago." On the other end, the guy replied, "Umm . . . YES?" That was the first red flag. Call me soft, but I think a "My condolences" wouldn't have killed anyone at that point. Then he told me he needed to get a pencil and was gone for an oddly long time. Another red flag was that it took four minutes to spell my father's first name to him. It's not like it's one of those long, multisyllabic names. It's five letters: Faruq. At one point, the guy at the mosque spelled it back to me "S-A- . . ." and I said, "No. Not Saruq. He wasn't from Middle Earth. *F*. *F* as in Frank. Or since we're both Muslims, *F* . . . AS IN FARUQ!" There was a King Farouk who ruled Egypt. There is a city in Pakistan called Farooqabad (literally, the place of Farooq). The prophet Muhammad's father-in-law was known by the epithet "al-Farooq." Come on, man, work with me here! (I later looked up Saruq. It's a Jewish last name, of all things.)

The day after this call, with my faith in the system shaky at best, I went to the mosque in person to put my heart at ease, to ensure that my father's body would actually arrive there the next day for his own funeral. It was only once I got there that I realized any "ensuring" came down to me saying, "There won't be ANY problem with his body arriving on time, will there?" and getting the response "No, brazzher, zere won't be no broblem." My English professor dad would have been sorely disappointed at the grammatical quality of that response. In the end, that transport was the one thing that happened flawlessly—probably because, I'm sad to say, it was arranged by a French fu-neral transportation company. Given Dad's weird bias against the French, I'm not sure he would have found that particularly funny.

My dad's friend (hereafter referred to as Uncle) was with me, and he grew upset about why Dad's body couldn't be in an Islamic environment (the mosque) for the night, instead of at the hospital morgue. A conversation with the imam was in order.

"Why don't you bring the body here?"
"No. We have no place to put it."
"We are supposed to have three fridges for bodies."
"No, we only have one." (My dad only needed one, so I had to assume that one was taken.)
"But two years ago, we raised money for two more fridges!"

And then there was an awkward silence that included a stare-down from Uncle to the imam. In sales, they say that in these moments the person who speaks first "loses." I guess Uncle lost, since he grew impatient with the silence on the imam's part and simply said, "Fine, I'll ask the other imam when I see him."

This mosque was the only one in the city that had these facilities. How-ever, I hear now that two other mosques will soon be installing fridges and facilities to wash and hold bodies. We'll see if competition helps this particular segment of the community.

Muslim funerals don't allow for speeches. It's not that they don't permit them, it's just that they are typically on a tight, focused schedule to get a per-son's body into the ground and on to its next and final destination. Simply put, it's just not done. Personally, I've always loved hearing people pay tribute to the deceased. If not at the actual funeral, then at the very least, something in the spirit of an Irish wake has always been appealing—lean into the pain, but also into the love you had for the person who is gone. And maybe lean into some sandwiches.

At the mosque on the day of my father's funeral, I sat on the ground—as is customary—with my back against the side wall, away from the rest of the congregation—which is *not* customary. And I stayed put there even when I was called forward by the imam to come help lead the prayer for my dad. Not just because of my inflexible joints and rusty memory for the prayer, but also because I pictured my dad laughing at me, saying, "You? Praying? Come off it!" It confused some of the people in attendance to no end that a son declined to lead the prayer for his dead father, but they seemed to chalk it up to "inconsolable grief" and moved on. My main thought, as I sat back and listened to the prayer in a language I still didn't speak or understand, was that this was an event begging for better speeches.

As a professor and a poet who surrounded himself with other professors and poets, my dad knew people who were well-trained in the art of public speaking. Their opportunity to speak at the funeral, alas, did not come. But mine did. At an "in memoriam" event hosted at Dawson College, my dad's friends and colleagues gathered to fondly remember him. I took the opportunity to say a few words. It was a speech that I titled "Faruq Hassan: The Luckiest Man I Ever Knew."

> When I was a young boy, whenever my friends were over at our house and would politely ask my dad, "How are you, Mr. Hassan?" we could be sure to hear one of his stock answers: "Oh, still around," or "Still kicking." I remember how grim I found that response, especially compared to the answers I would get from my friends' fathers, and particularly juxtapositioned against his own Muslim family's "*Subhanallahs*" and "*Alhamdulillahs*" (roughly translating to "I am thankful to be alive, by the good grace of God"). But his lackadaisical answer belied an undeniable truth: my father was the luckiest man I knew.
>
> Well, maybe "lucky" is too strong. But I can say this: no one came out of a bad situation better than Faruq Hassan. Like the time he lost a finger after poking around near the car fan belt while a mechanic started the car—luckily it was on his left

hand, or his writing and translating career would have been devastated. Or the time they found a tumour in his lung—luckily it was removed, and he was completely spared the pain and exhaustion of radiation and chemotherapy. Or like his recoveries from angina, a heart attack, or a heart bypass. Each subsequent surgery or procedure was always a success, and he was up and back to his usual tricks—or some variation thereof—after each of those episodes. And of course, let us not forget the dozens and dozens of emergency room visits over the years for heart palpitations, or shortness of breath, or some other potentially frightening symptoms. I always marvelled at that trifecta of modern medicine (supplying him, at one point, with no less than twelve pills per day), his incredible will to live, and his undeniable luck that always collaborated to have him bouncing back from whatever ailed him.

When all these health scares are combined with the, shall we say, "juvenile behaviour" (I remember wondering if it was normal for my father to be regularly coming home after his teenage son. And how was he getting up for his 7:30 a.m. office hours?!) and the subsequent late, and less-than-alert drives home in Montreal (and previously New Brunswick) winters, I still find it just shy of a miracle that my father was able to be with us for seventy-two years. I mean, God's handiwork had to have been involved in some way.

His colleague Friedl once told me, "Ali, your father doesn't suffer fools gladly." Being too young at the time to fully appreciate what that meant, I thought it was something that reflected poorly on my father. As I watched him through the years, I realized quite the opposite. He simply chose not to spend his life associating with people who weren't appealing to him. But even if he was a little picky about his friends, he rarely—if ever—made enemies. He simply chose to distance himself from people in whom he wasn't interested. And that was the essence of my father: surrounding himself with people and activities he enjoyed. As a corollary, anything he didn't enjoy (e.g., carefully managing his money) wouldn't get his attention, either. He was a lively, witty, and charming man whose life was full of so many contradictions. He was a stingy marker, but an incredibly generous man; he was a notorious procrastinator, but accomplished so much; he had a foul mouth at times, but he preached proper English usage all the time; he was irreligious, but incorruptible; he took poor care of his health and yet had a powerful desire to live; and finally, although he enjoyed being foolish, Friedl nailed it, he didn't suffer fools.

In the very end, there was no suffering, period. His brain was unable to feel any pain or anything at all, really, for the last two weeks of his life. That was definitely the hardest part for his family—seeing him in that neuro-vegetative state. It was the one thing that really broke all our hearts. We could all agree that he polluted his lungs and clogged his arteries, but his mind . . . Oh, how he nourished that mind. In retirement, his day only began after he read both the *Globe and Mail* and the *Montreal Gazette*. His voracious reading appetite and borderline speed-reading allowed him to read a few books a week. Right until his last days, he was actively translating poems and short stories into Urdu, Persian, and Arabic. Although nothing can replace his loss, I still feel this unusual sense of gratitude that I've never felt before. I'm so grateful that I knew him and that he was around as long as he was. And I'm so grateful that he got to see me pursuing my own professional dreams and had the chance to meet my loving wife, my two daughters, and his two-month-old grandson before his body called it quits.

On his last day, he went painlessly and peacefully, weeks or maybe months ahead of certain hospitalization that we were told would have included having a tracheotomy or spending his remaining days on a respirator. I'm certain that Dad himself would have thought his luck was about to run out. But God, or the Universe, or something, intervened, and helped him hightail it out of here before he needed to go down that path of certain misery. A final lucky break for the luckiest man I ever knew.

When I was a little kid, the image that I had of God was always one of a white man with a long-flowing beard, draped in an eggshell-white toga, looking down at me from above the clouds. So basically, Santa Claus meets Zeus. Minimal though my Sunday school learnings might have been, they certainly began to test that image of God. Why would he need to be white, when so much of the world wasn't? When he spoke to the angels or Adam and Eve, did he have an accent? Why did he need to be high in the sky if he was, as I was taught, omnipresent and omnipotent? Also, was he watching me in the bathroom right now? Like, how present *is* omnipresent, anyway?

Over my life, I would have many ups and downs with Islam—doubting it, questioning it, eschewing it completely, returning to it with interest, leaving it again in dismay, and coming back to it after 9/11 (because what other choice did I really have?)—until I finally made my peace with my identity in my mid-thirties. During this entire time, I never knew my father to struggle with his concept of God or Islam, even the slightest. He knew who he was. He knew what the religion was. And he knew his place within it.

Religious scholar Huston Smith wrote that the Sufis are the mystics of Islam and that "every upright Muslim expects to see God after death, but the Sufis are the impatient ones. They want God now—moment by moment, day by day, in this very life." My father, as I suggested in the eulogy, lived every day to its fullest. Perhaps a little too full, but that was his way. He was also as real as they come. To be phony or artificial in any way would be a waste of time, reduce life's enjoyment, and be very un-Sufi-like. I'd like to believe that he passed these traits on to me, although I exercise them with a little bit more balance.

And while I have none of the discipline of a practising Sufi, I certainly have all the impatience. Even the two most soul-satisfying careers I found were grounded in *instant* gratification. In the food world, you know very soon if your meal is well received—you just have to wait for the hopefully empty plates to come back to the kitchen. In comedy, it's even faster. The joke should be, ideally, immediately followed by laughter (although many a comedian has consoled themselves by thinking, *Hmm . . . they didn't like it now, but they'll get it on the drive home*).

I have found that gratitude has kept me, day by day, connected to God. Being thankful, being grateful—this is what has helped me find my "sweet spot," smack-dab in the middle of the spectrum between the orthodox practitioners of Islam and the complete atheists. And I find myself grateful so often, for so much—my wife, my family, my wife's family, my friends, my career, my lot in life—that I imagine God, if he were to look down at me in his toga, to say, "Give it a rest, Hassan. I get it. You're grateful."

In the big bed of religion, I rolled around way too much, had some really fitful sleeps, and even broke a few of the springs in the mattress and the slats that held it up! But my hope for my kids is that they sleep comfortably, with some confidence, knowing who they are and where to look for support. The way I am inspired by them to be positive about the future, I hope I can inspire them, too, to be grateful and trusting in the general goodness in the world, despite all the bad stuff happening.

When you mention "inheritance" in this day and age, the average person's mind will turn to the financial, tangible stuff you get when a relative or parent passes away. My dad died the same way he lived: broke. But because he was an English teacher, there were *a lot* of office supplies left behind. Possibly contraband, we didn't ask too many questions. So many office supplies were left behind, in fact, that even when I'm long gone, my children's children will never want for a staple or an envelope for as long as they live. More important, my father also left a model for decency. While he may not have suffered fools, he was never out to scam, or lie, or cheat anyone. This is what I now have to pass on to my kids. And in the absence of religious training, this is what I turn to for my lessons to my children:

Be positive.

Be grateful.

And pull out a page from my Sunday school playbook of all places: be kind, be merciful, and be forgiving.

Live with love and acceptance, and hopefully you'll have a rewarding and satisfying life. Inshallah.

EPILOGUE

A FEW THINGS HAPPENED DURING the period that I was writing this book. The first was a reality check about my health. The second was an unprecedented worldwide pandemic (you probably heard about that one). And third were the deaths of my friend Vikram and my mother.

In March 2020, an old friend from my McGill University days surprised me backstage at my final performance of *Muslim, Interrupted* at the Aga Khan Museum in Toronto. It was a few minutes until showtime, and we quickly caught up: he had lived in the US Midwest for medical training, he'd been in Boston working as a geneticist for a few years, and was now back in Toronto setting up a family medicine practise. Where? It turned out his new clinic was across the street from my neighbourhood! It felt incredibly serendipitous. I needed a new family doctor, and here I was meeting this old physician friend who could've lived anywhere in the greater Toronto area, but he was a block away from my house? This had to be my new guy!

Unfortunately, "my guy" was quickly the bearer of much bad news. I'll spare you the metrics, but suffice it to say that the results from my initial blood work—around my blood sugar, cholesterol, and liver—were seriously concerning. And it turned out I had gout. I had gotten what they call "the rich man's disease"—without going through the "getting rich" part. My background, my genes, and my lifestyle had all caught up with me.

My father had always approached his health the same way he approached his car troubles: *There's a weird sound coming from the car engine? Turn up the radio! There's a pain in my chest? Drink more so as not to think about it!* But I knew better. And I had to do better. Sticking around to see my children grow up seemed much cooler than going out with a "He died doing what he loved: eating two pounds of chicken wings and drinking a half-priced pitcher."

Under the guidance of this new doctor, I made some pretty drastic changes. I transitioned to eating a plant-based diet, for six days a week. Instead of "meatless Monday," I did meat-full Sundays. So, if you were concerned about my pork consumption—for religious or health reasons—you'll be happy (or outraged) to know that I've essentially "kicked the habit." And since what followed March 2020 was a pandemic, I basically ate at home with my family (anti-porkers) and simply managed to avoid pork for quite some time.

The pandemic was oddly beneficial for my health, and for the closeness of my family. We were eating well, exercising, and catching up on ground-breaking television programming like *90 Day Fiancé.* My boys were still young enough that they looked at my wife and me and said, "Wait a minute—we get to stay home from school *and* we get to hang with you guys? This is awesome!" For my daughters—well, imagine if *you* were forced to stay home with your parents when you were a teenager. It wasn't always ideal for them, but we all tried to make the most of it.

Where things floundered was in the comedy department. Performances were on hiatus indefinitely. They'd come back for a few months, and just as comedians were getting some momentum and rhythm, we'd go into a lock-down again. Sure, there were Zoom shows, but call me crazy—performing to the green dot on my laptop screen didn't yield quite the same joy as live audiences did.

And, if a virus transmissible by one's mouth mist that hospitalized and killed people by the hundreds of thousands wasn't bad enough, the horror of this time was further amplified by events like the murder of George Floyd. I can't explain how hard it is to write a comedic memoir about your once-confusing but ultimately happy, second-generation immigrant life after watching the worst of police brutality on the Black community.

I was finally, with the help and encouragement of my editor, able to get into the rhythm of writing again, until April 2021. That is when our tight-knit group of friends from Montreal had our world completely rocked. Our friend Vikram suffered a horrific reaction from his first vaccine, which led to a blood clot in his brain. He became, and remains, the one person in the province of Ontario to die from vaccine-related thrombosis. He was my back-door neighbour in Brossard for many years, he was a lover of good food like no one else I knew, a soul music lover, a man with a zest for life and a love for family. We teased him for being unfairly handsome, intelligent, and charming. And he was taken from us so damned abruptly, leaving behind a wife and two children. It felt devastatingly unfair and always will.

Two days hadn't passed since the tragedy of Vikram's passing, and we got another piece of startling news. The tentacles of COVID ran deep and affected so many people, and sadly my mother was also not an exception. Mom was a woman who had always trusted her doctors and the medical community at large, but during the pandemic couldn't get in to see anyone for her various chest pains for many months. At most, she would get a phone call with her family doctor. Had it not been for the pandemic, and the various people who prolonged it, I believe my mother would have been diagnosed with her cancer in stage 1 or 2. Instead, she could hardly see a doctor in person for close to a year, and when she did, the appointments were brusque. While she tried for several months to ease her pains with Advil and hot-water bottles, we finally got the news: stage 4 lymphoma. It was baffling. A woman of moderation her entire life—never drank, smoke, or even overate—diagnosed with stage 4 cancer. Four months after that diagnosis my mother passed. Killed ultimately by the chemotherapy that we all had hoped would cure her.

Recently my own family was struck with COVID. Levelled, one by one. And I couldn't help but miss my mother immensely. Not because I needed my mother's tenderness, exactly, but more because my mother always had suggestions when anyone was sick. They varied from conventional medication to ginger tea to nasal "irrigation." And she was always there to call whenever I had questions about the family, or if anyone was getting married or had departed this world. She was also, particularly in her later years, always ready with information and advice about Islam. With her gone, *I* am now the authority on Islam for my family. Jesus wept.

During the time that I wrote this book, I have gotten more life experience than I could have imagined, but my hope is that it made for a more honest piece of work.

ACKNOWLEDGEMENTS

IN THE WRITING OF THIS BOOK, I have found there are three types of people in my life: those who are very supportive and congratulatory, those who have no idea what I'm doing with my time (*"You're writing a memoir?"*), and those who respond with "You're too young to be writing a memoir!"

To that last group, I say the following: Firstly, you are vastly overestimating the power of my memory. God only knows what I'll be able to recall a decade from now! And secondly, did you read the book? I'm a South Asian man with heart disease and diabetes looming over my head, whose parents were first cousins—things could go south at any moment! In the spirit of the old saying "smoke 'em if you got 'em," I say, *Write it if you have it!*

This book grew out of a stage show that I performed for four years, entitled *Muslim, Interrupted*. Both the show and this book would never have taken shape without the help of so many people, to whom I am truly indebted.

To my touring agent, Aaron Schubert, thank you for pushing my live show across this country and giving me the confidence to tell these stories to large groups of people. To my film and television agent, Ryan Goldhar—and his indispensable right hand, Karen Kane—thank you for your guidance, and for somehow always making me feel like I'm your one and only client. Tara Mora and Ann MacKeigan, thank you for taking a chance on me, introducing me to a whole new world, and turning me into the "small-b" broadcaster that I am. To Tracy Rideout, "a special thanks to my producer." I shudder to think where I'd be without your support and championing.

ACKNOWLEDGEMENTS

Qurram Hussain, Asif Doja, Hasan Alam, Azim Hussain—thank you all for your contributions to this book and my life over the years, and for always being so enthusiastic in my impromptu brainstorming sessions. Arsalaan Hyder, like Batman you appear and then disappear into the shadows, but when you are around, you have always inspired me to think hard and write well. Dave Merheje, thank you for inspiring me always, in ways you wouldn't even know about. Amir Rizk, thank you for pushing me constantly to get to the meat of the funny. Our months and months of unremunerated work were a masterclass of training in voice work, character development, and script writing.

My wife—God only knows what you were thinking when you took a chance on a guy working the open-mic comedy circuit and prepping catering gigs out of his parents' garage, but I'll be eternally grateful that you did. Thank you also for giving me the time, space, and encouragement to write this. My children—in many ways, this memoir is for you. I look forward to you reading it, and then submitting a book report back to me. Thanks for making our family a fun and rewarding one to be part of. I feel proud to go to work for all of you.

To my sister, Naurooz, thank you for choosing not to hold any grudges against your temperamental brother. And to my late parents—confused and dismayed though they may have been with their son for many years—their home was always my home. And their money, if they had any extra, was my money. They may not have understood or even liked my dreams at times, but they were uniquely instrumental in helping me chase them and realize them.

If this was a live awards show, the music would be playing me off now, but there are two very important people left to thank. This book exists because of Dan French and my editor, Justin Stoller. Dan firmly planted the idea in my mind that my stage show could and should be a book. Of course, he neglected to mention that it required hundreds of hours of work on top of that, but I digress. He also introduced me to Justin, who, with the patience of a Buddhist monk, assembled and crafted my collection of disjointed ramblings into the book you see before you. Thank you from the bottom of my heart for your tireless work.

So, now you know who to blame if you didn't care for the book. But for all of you who over the years booked me, cast me, hired me, laughed with me, encouraged me, supported me, and celebrated any of my work—thanks for being part of this crazy journey.